Christ at the centre
Selected Issues in Christology

Dermot A. Lane

VERITAS

1990

First published 1990 by
Veritas Publications
7–8 Lr Abbey Street
Dublin 1

Copyright © Dermot A. Lane 1990

ISBN I 85390 101 6

Nihil Obstat
Thomas Norris
Censor deputatis

The publishers are grateful to the following for permission to use
extracts from their copyright material:
Brendan Kennelly for 'Willow'; Editions de Minuit and Georges
Borchardt Inc. for *Night* by Elie Wiesel; extracts from the *Revised
Standard Version* of the Bible, copyright 1946, 1952, 1971 by the
Division of Christian Education of the National Council of the Churches
of Christ in the USA. Excerpt from 'Dry Salvages' in *Four Quartets*
copyright 1943 by T. S. Eliot and renewed 1971 by Esmé Valerie Eliot,
reprinted by permission of Harcourt Brace Jovanovich Inc. and Faber &
Faber Ltd.

Cover design by Banahan McManus, Dublin
Typesetting by Printset & Design Ltd, Dublin
Printed in the Republic of Ireland by Mount Salus Press Ltd

CONTENTS

Acknowledgements

The putting together of a book is a curious and complex affair. It is never quite simply the work of the author alone, though there are many long and lonely hours spent in deciding finally what for better or worse stays in. The environment of one's work also shapes the final outcome of the text.

My immediate environment has been happily one of teaching students of theology in Mater Dei Institute of Education and Holy Cross College in Dublin. I wish, therefore, to record my thanks in the first instance to the students in both of these colleges for their stimulating questions which helped me to sharpen my own thinking. I am also grateful to the many colleagues whose conversations have been a great source of inspiration and nourishment. Then there are my family and friends whose support and encouragement helped to keep the project going in all kinds of ways, often unknown to them.

In particular I wish to thank Sr Bernard Boran, Revv. Bill Cosgrave, Jim Dollard and Bill Riley, who generously read sections of the book and made constructive suggestions for its improvement.

A special word of thanks must go to Mrs Maura Purcell, Secretary to Mater Dei Institute, who word-processed many different drafts with great patience and skill.

Finally, quotations from the Bible are taken from the *Revised Standard Version,* Catholic Edition, 1966, and references to the documents of the Second Vatican Council are taken from the 1966 Walter Abbot Edition.

Introduction

The centre of the gospel and the life of the Church is the living person, Jesus of Nazareth, crucified and risen, confessed as the Christ, the Son of God and the Saviour of the world, ιχθυζ. Being a christian is about being a disciple of Jesus and this involves a commitment in action to the person of Jesus and to everything that he stood for: the Reign of God, the love of God and neighbour, solidarity with the poor, reconciliation and justice for all. The purpose of this book is to highlight some – not all – of the important issues that Jesus personally embodied in his life: good news, freedom, the cross, the resurrection, the personal presence of God in the human condition. In particular, *Christ at the Centre* seeks to bridge the gap between what theologians are saying about Jesus today and what christians in the pews believe. Consequently this book does not pretend to be original nor does it claim to break new ground. More modestly, it aims to mediate a dialogue between scholarship and discipleship, between human experience and the commitment of faith, and between contemporary interpretation and the christian tradition. To this extent the book is addressed to adult christians, religious educators, ministers of the gospel, and students of theology.

More and more theology is becoming christocentric. Everything in the christian faith is, or should be, related in one way or another to the person of Christ. Whether we are talking about the Church or the sacraments or God or the end of the world, reference must be made to Christ. For example, the Church is the community of people who gather to confess and celebrate the Lordship of Jesus; the sacraments are about the liberating and saving activity of Christ in the world; the awesome reality of God is made visible in the personal life of Jesus; the apocalyptic end of the world has been prefigured in the violent death and glorious resurrection of Jesus.

These different aspects of the christian mystery are developed in the pages that follow.

Even though the person of Christ is at the centre of the christian faith, it is often pointed out by critics both inside and outside the christian tradition that Christ is not always clearly to the fore. For example, Frederick Nietzsche makes the disturbing observation that 'Christianity is the tombstone over the grave of Jesus'. Alfred N. Whitehead in a few tantalising but undeveloped lines claims that 'The brief Galilean vision of humility flickered throughout the ages...But the deeper idolatry, of the fashioning of God in the image of Egyptian, Persian, and Roman imperial rulers, was retained. The Church gave unto God the attributes which belong exclusively to Caesar.'[1] Jon Sobrino charges that 'the reality of Christ, his person, has been manipulated, distorted, commandeered, "kidnapped" '.[2] M. Gandhi once remarked 'I like your Christ but not his followers'. The Extraordinary Synod of Bishops in Rome celebrating the twentieth anniversary of Vatican II in 1985 observes in a sentence of striking candour 'The Church becomes more credible if it speaks less about itself and more and more preaches Christ crucified (1 Co 2:2) and witnesses to Him by its life'.[3] These observations and others have prompted a return to the foundations of our faith in Christ.

At the same time we need to remember that in trying to recover the centrality of Christ at the end of this century it is impossible simply to lift Christ out of the gospels and transpose him into the twentieth century. The Christ of the gospels and the christian tradition is a Christ already interpreted in the light of the christian community's experiences and needs. The person of Christ in scripture and tradition, though universal in appeal, exists only as embedded in a particular cultural matrix. In trying to communicate Christ today account must be taken of our peculiar and particular cultural matrix. Part of that cultural matrix today includes realities like feminism, the new cosmologies, the quest for wholeness, the

1 *Process in Reality*, Corrected Edition, New York: The Free Press, 1978, p. 342.
2 Jon Sobrino, *Jesus in Latin America*, New York: Orbis Books, 1987, p. 12.
3 *Synod Report: The Final Report and Message to the People of God*, London: CTS, 1986, section A2.

struggle for justice, peace and the integrity of creation. The pages that follow try to take some account of these contemporary cultural issues in critical correlation with the mystery of Christ.

This book also sets out to shed some light for people and priests on the great historical events that all christians celebrate liturgically each year in Holy Week and Eastertide. Though many will be familiar with the language of the cross, the resurrection and the paschal mystery, there is a pastoral need to spell out the theological richness of these realities. For too long liturgy and christology seem to have gone their own independent ways. The time is now ripe for a new conversation between christology and liturgy with a view to enhancing the relationship between commitment and worship in the lives of people. It is hoped that some of the issues raised in this book will help to stimulate a dialogue between christology and liturgy.

As the churches face into a new decade and prepare for a new century as well as a new millennium with new questions, they will be forced to return to the source of their origins in the paschal mystery of the historical life, death and resurrection of Jesus. Indeed, the credibility of the churches in the future will be judged by their ability to embody in faith and praxis the healing mission and ministry of Jesus in the world today.

This book is written in the faith and conviction that in the end Christ 'is the goal of human history, the focal point of the longings of history and of civilisation, the centre of the human race, the joy of every heart and the answer to all its yearnings'.[4] It is hoped that something of that faith and conviction will be communicated in the chapters that follow.

Finally, *Christ at the Centre: Selected Issues in Christology* seeks to complement – not replace – my earlier work entitled *The Reality of Jesus: an Essay in Christology,* Dublin/New York: Veritas Publications/Paulist Press 1975. *The Reality of Jesus* stands on its own independent feet as an introductory text to the biblical, patristic and theological aspects of the mystery of Christ. In contrast, *Christ*

---

4   *Pastoral Constitution on the Church in the Modern World,* 1965 a. 45.

at the Centre tries to develop in more detail issues that were raised only in passing in *The Reality of Jesus*. These issues include the biblical and theological meaning of the Reign of God, the revelation of a crucified God on the cross of Jesus, an experiential approach to the resurrection, an outline of the structures of the paschal mystery and its significance for christian life today, and an attempt to talk about the cosmic significance of the incarnation.

Holy Week 1990   Dermot A. Lane
                        Mater Dei Institute of Education
                        Dublin

1

Jesus and the Reign of God: Biblical Perspectives

The Kingdom of God, or what many prefer to call the Reign of God, is at the centre of the preaching of Jesus. Indeed everything that Jesus says and does is inspired from beginning to end by his personal commitment to the coming Reign of God into the world. The controlling horizon of the mission and ministry of Jesus is the Kingdom of God. The life, death and resurrection of Jesus derive their meaning from the announcement of the Kingdom of God.

Even a passing acquaintance with the gospels reveals the prominence of the Kingdom in the life of Jesus. Most of the parables are stories about the Kingdom in one form or another and nearly all the miracles are signs of the coming of the Kingdom into the world. On a purely statistical level we find the Reign of God/heaven *(basileia tou theou/ton ouranon)* occurs well over a hundred times in the synoptic gospels whereas explicit reference to the Church appears only in two passages in the synoptics. Yet, as we shall see, an indissoluble link exists between the Kingdom and the Church.

In spite of this centrality of the Reign of God in the life of Jesus, the Kingdom has not always been to the fore either in christology or christian theology down through the centuries. There are different reasons for this. For one thing, the Church gradually moved to the centre of the stage early on in the life of christianity. Further, the alliance between Church and state under Constantine in the fourth century became an added impetus for concentration on the Church. In addition, Augustine's important and influential work *The City of*

God (425), which has much to say about the Kingdom of God, tends towards identifying the Church with the Reign of God. In effect what happened during the early centuries was that the Reign of God as preached by Jesus gradually receded from christian consciousness once christianity moved into the Greco-Roman world. Why? Mainly because the philosophical and cultural suppositions of the Greco-Roman world were more inclined towards an emphasis on spiritual salvation and the personal immortality of the individual soul, and less sympathetic to the social and holistic dimensions of salvation represented by the symbol of the Reign of God in the New Testament.[1] As one author observes 'the advent of the Kingdom of God was soon replaced in christianity by a spiritualised and individualistic hope for immortal, celestial life'.[2]

An additional reason why the meaning of the Reign of God is so difficult to grasp is because it is a multi-layered symbol in contrast to a single-layered symbol. Multi-layered symbols (sometimes called 'tensive-symbols') have a wide range of meaning that cannot be exhausted by any one referent, whereas a single-layered symbol (sometimes called 'steno-symbols') has only a one-to-one relationship to that which it represents.[3] As a multi-layered symbol the Reign of God as proclaimed by Jesus has at least theological, christological, ecclesiological, ecological, and eschatological import.

Thus we find the Reign of God assuming a new importance in contemporary theology, especially in the newly-emerging political and liberation theologies. However, before the Reign of God can be fully re-appropriated in the rest of christian theology we need to recover its centrality in christology.

The purpose of this opening chapter is to outline the biblical background to the Reign of God and to examine its centrality in the life of Jesus.

---

1 A good account of this change can be found in B.T. Viviano in *The Kingdom of God in History*, Delaware: Michael Glazier, 1988, ch. 2.
2 J.M. Bonino, *Doing Theology in a Revolutionary Situation*, Philadelphia: Fortress Press, 1975, p. 133.
3 N. Perrin, *Jesus and the Language of the Kingdom*, Philadelphia: Fortress Press, 1976 pp. 29-30. The distinction between 'steno-symbols' and 'tensive-symbols' goes back to the work of P. Wheelwright, *Metaphor and Reality*, Bloomington, Indiana: University Press, 1962, pp. 92-96.

The Reign of God in the Religion of Israel

When we look at the preaching of Jesus concerning the Reign of God, we notice immediately that he was using a term already existing in the symbolic vocabulary of his audience. The disciples appear to be reasonably familiar with the symbol of the Reign of God, even though much of the teaching of Jesus is given to correcting distortions that had crept into this ancient symbol. To appreciate the preaching of Jesus we need to take some account of the Jewish background to the Reign of God.

When we turn to the pre-christian scriptures we discover that the expression 'the Kingdom of God' does not appear in the Hebrew scriptures with the exception of Wisdom 10:10. However, ideas about the rule and sovereignty of Yahweh, about God as King and Lord are found throughout the Hebrew scriptures and as such are an important part of the background to the preaching of Jesus. These ideas of the kingship, lordship, and sovereignty of Yahweh in turn are derived from the peculiarly Jewish understanding of the activity of Yahweh in history, in creation, and in the period of the monarchy.

Within Judaism there was a long-standing, deep-seated faith in the activity of Yahweh in the history of the people of Israel. Pre-eminent here was the activity of Yahweh in those historical events that resulted in the liberation of the people from slavery in Egypt, giving rise to their formation into a distinct entity known as Israel. This personal involvement of Yahweh is not something that is simply confined to the exodus event but also forms part of Israel's interpretation of other key moments in her history such as journeying in the wilderness, the setting up of the Sinai Covenant, entry into the promised land, the creation of the monarchy, the exile and the return from exile. Within this complicated history of the people of Israel there is a keen sense of the providential and reigning presence of Yahweh leading, guiding, and shaping their history. This sense of Yahweh as personally active in the history of Israel is powerfully portrayed in the Deuteronomic creed:

> A wandering Aramean was my father, and he went down into Egypt... and the Egyptians treated us harshly, and afflicted us...

> Then we cried to the Lord the God of our fathers, and the Lord heard our voice, and saw our affliction, our toil, and our oppression; and the Lord brought us out of Egypt with a mighty hand ... and he brought us into this place and gave us this land, a land flowing with milk and honey (Dt 26:5-9, see also Ex 3:7-12).

Though it is a matter of some dispute as to whether Yahweh is explicitly called king before or after the monarchy, there can be little doubt that it is Israel's awareness of God's active presence in their history that enables them to understand God as King:

> The Lord will reign for ever and ever (Ex 15:18).

What is central and distinctive within the Israelite religion is that their history is governed by Yahweh, that Yahweh is always present to the people of Israel in their history, and that therefore history does have a purpose and goal, even if this purpose and goal seem to change from time to time. This Israelite perspective is an important element in arriving at a proper understanding of what it means to talk about the coming Reign of God as the goal of history.

Another equally significant ingredient in the Kingship and Lordship of God is the Israelite understanding of Yahweh as Creator. While it is true to say that the Israelite religion was influenced by the creation myths of surrounding cultures, nonetheless it did come up with its own distinct perception of God as Creator. The immediate background to the creation story of Genesis portraying God as Creator is the conquest by Yahweh of the primeval forces of chaos at the beginning of time. It was through this conquest that Yahweh established the order of the cosmos and ensured the fertility of creation through the different seasons of the year. Out of this mix of ideas came a particular perception of Yahweh as Lord of creation. Shades of this understanding of Yahweh as Creator are captured in some of the enthronement Psalms of Israelite worship:

> The Lord reigns; he is robed in majesty; the Lord is robed, he is girded with strength. Yea, the world is established; it shall never be moved; thy throne is established from of old; thou art from everlasting (Ps 93:1-2; see also Pss 47, 93, 97).

Another good example of the Israelite understanding that Yahweh, as Creator and Lord of all the earth, is the worthy subject of worship can be found in Psalm 96:

> O sing to the Lord a new song, sing to the Lord, all the earth. Say among the nations, the Lord reigns. Yea, the world is established, it shall never be moved (Ps 96:1,10).

These two traditions about the presence of Yahweh in history and the activity of Yahweh as creator gradually come together over a period of time in a mutually enriching synthesis. The act of creation by God at the beginning of time is forwarded to include the activity of God in the salvation history of Israel. Likewise the activity of God in the history of salvation is projected back to embrace creation. The God who is author of the exodus experience and the covenant relationship is also at the same time the one God who is Lord of creation. The synthesis of these two separate traditions influences the Israelite understanding of the kingship, lordship and sovereignty of Yahweh.

Another factor shaping the biblical symbol of the rule of God is the experience of the monarchy – described by one author as 'a major impulse'.[4] The Deuteronomistic account portrays the establishment of the monarchy as something undertaken with considerable reluctance in Israel. On the one hand the establishment of the monarchy is something of a pragmatic necessity to cope with political threats and pressures from outside. On the other hand it is presented as something fraught with ambiguity in virtue of the centrality of monotheism in the Israelite religion and the strong allegiance to the absolute sovereignty of the one true God that this implies. One particular speech of Samuel shows awareness of the abuses that can arise from a centralised authority vested in the person of the king (1 S 8:10-18), albeit *post-factum* in origin. The authority of the king, as elsewhere in the ancient near East, must be limited by the absolute sovereignty of God. None the less the earthly king is authorised to act in the name of Yahweh *vis-à-vis* his people.

4 D. Senior, 'The Reign of God', *The New Dictionary of Theology*, J. Komanchak, M. Collins, D. Lane (eds.), Delaware: Michael Glazier, 1987, p. 853.

The period of the monarchy, often over-idealised in the biblical tradition, gave Israel a strong sense of her own identity and destiny. While in theory that sense of identity and destiny is derived ultimately from the kingship and sovereignty of God, all too often the history of the monarchy and its kings who were intended to represent Yahweh is scarred by human failure and compromise in loyalty. Yet, the greatness of Israel and the promise of greatness in the future begin to find particular expression in and through the experience of the monarchy. It is through David, and his offspring, that God will establish Israel as a mighty nation in the future:

> When your days are fulfilled and you lie down with your ancestors, I will raise up your offspring after you, who shall come forth from your body, and I will establish his kingdom. He shall build a house for my name, and I will establish the throne of his kingdom for ever. I will be his father and he shall be my son (2 S 7:12-14).

The subsequent history of Israel, which sees the break-up of the monarchy in terms of exile and later a return from exile, is interpreted within Judaism as ongoing aspects of God's reign and rule over his people and his creational sovereignty. The period of the exile is understood by the prophets as one of divine judgment and the period of return as an act of divine forgiveness. In both instances, God continues to exercise a historical sovereignty/kingship and a creation-based lordship over his people. During the period of the exile and the return from exile concrete hopes for the Reign of God begin to take shape. These hopes are expressed by the prophets; they are historical in character and are therefore principally this-worldly in outlook. For example, Deutero-Isaiah talks explicitly about the liberation of Israel from exile in ways that parallel the liberation of Israel from Egypt:

> Thus says the Lord, your redeemer, the holy one of Israel: for your sake I will send to Babylon and break down all the bars, and the shouting of Chaldeans will be turned to lamentations. I am the Lord, your holy one, the creator of Israel, your king ... Behold I am doing a new thing; now it springs forth, do you not perceive it? I will make a way in the wilderness and rivers in the desert (Is 43:14-19).

These historical hopes, partly as a result of their failure and partly

because of a deepening awareness of the full theological significance of God's covenant with Israel, are followed by the development of other-worldly eschatological hopes which find expression in
the late apocalyptic literature of Judaism:

> And in the days of those kings, the God of heaven will set up a
> kingdom which shall never be destroyed, nor shall its sovereignty be
> left to another people (Dn 2:44, see also Dn 12:1-4).

The coming together of these three themes, namely God's activity
in history, God's presence in creation, and the historical experience
of the monarchy and the temple, make up the basic ingredients of
an incipient theology of the Reign of God in the pre-christian
scriptures. While God is always one and utterly transcendent, God is
also at the same time actively present in history and in creation as
Lord and King, governing the lives of his people, and leading them
into a new future. This perception of the kingship and lordship of
God relativises the authority of all purely human, political and
religious figures. Jewish monotheism, with its emphasis on the
sovereignty of God, symbolises a kind of opposition to earthly
authorities and kings. At the same time this understanding of God
generates a hope for the future and this hope is both a this-worldly
(largely pre-exilic) and an other-worldly (mainly post-exilic) hope.
Judaism looks to the future for the fulfilment of the historical hopes
brought about by the liberating activity of the God who had
gathered them as a nation and sustained them as a people through a
history of mixed fortunes. In particular, Judaism in the Hellenistic
period looks to the future for the advent of a messianic figure,
sometimes expressed as a New Moses who will inaugurate the last
days, establish "the day of the Lord" and set up the liberating Reign
of Yahweh in the world.

A strong sense of prophetic and eschatological expectation
permeates the period preceding the advent of Jesus. This hope for
the coming Reign of God would have included liberation from the
oppressive Roman rule regulating the life of Israel in Palestine. After
all, God as King had delivered them historically in the past from
captivity in Egypt and therefore a part of their messianic expectation

now embraced a similar hope for freedom from Roman domination. Other elements which entered into the messianic expectation would have been the hope of lasting peace, some form of cosmic renewal, the setting up of a new covenant, and the establishment of the justice of God on earth. When these things would come to pass, then the full sovereignty of God would be re-established in Israel. This hoped-for state of affairs is summed up in a kaddish prayer in use in the synagogue just before the time of Jesus. It is worth quoting this prayer because it re-appears in modified form later on as part of the prayer of Jesus. The kaddish prayer in historical reconstruction runs as follows:

> Magnified and sanctified be his great name in the world...

> May he establish his kingdom in your lifetime and in your days and in the lifetime of all the house of Israel ...[5]

The Preaching and Praxis of Jesus

The preaching and praxis of Jesus should be situated in the context of this symbolic vision of God from the Hebrew scriptures, a vision which sees God as personally active in the history of Israel and continually present to his people in the processes of creation. This twofold doctrine about God in history and creation in turn has received a particular synthesis in the light of Israel's experience of the monarchy and the temple which, at the same time, informs the messianic hope. God as king and lord is guiding the history of Israel towards the goal of salvation: peace, justice and cosmic renewal in the particular context of great messianic expectations. Within this climate there was a significant variety of ways in which the sovereign rule of God on earth was expected to be established. For the Qumran community the Reign of God will be brought about through a form of passive waiting, withdrawal from public life, a rigorous asceticism and a final warfare of cosmic dimensions. For the Zealots, the rule of God will be ushered in by a political uprising and the use of violence. For the Pharisees, God's

5   Taken from N. Perrin, *Jesus and the Language of the Kingdom*, op. cit., p. 28.

sovereignty would come about through strict adherence to the Torah.

It was in the midst of these conflicting responses that:

> Jesus came into Galilee, preaching the gospel of God, saying 'the time is fulfilled, and the kingdom of God is at hand; repent and believe in the gospel' (Mk 1:14-15).

While this summary can hardly be taken to represent the historical words of Jesus, it does however capture the theological orientation of his message.

What does Jesus mean by saying 'the time is fulfilled'? The underlying assumption here is the Jewish apocalyptic view of history, namely that the goal of history under the guidance of God is drawing near, that the transition from the old age into the new age is somehow about to take place. This theme about the age of fulfilment plays an important part in the preaching of Jesus. For instance, Jesus can say after reading the Book of Isaiah in the synagogue at Nazareth:

> Today this scripture has been fulfilled in your hearing (Lk 4:21).

On another occasion Jesus says to his disciples:

> Blessed are the eyes which see what you see. For I tell you that many prophets and kings desired to see what you see and did not see it and to hear what you hear and did not hear it (Lk 10:23-24).

Clearly for Jesus there is a deep awareness that in and through his own person and proclamation an eschatological breakthrough from the old to the new is taking place.

It was this awareness of a special moment in history *(kairos)* that enabled Jesus to say 'The Kingdom of God is at hand' and mean by this that the sovereign Reign of God is nearby and close at hand. The power and presence of God in history and in creation is about to break into the world and become manifest in a way that will establish the absolute kingship and lordship of God. To vindicate this claim Jesus performed particular deeds that point towards the actual nearness of this coming Reign of God: healings, exorcisms, forgiveness, and a new table fellowship. Further, for Jesus to emphasise that the Reign of God 'is at hand' was to suggest that God is personally active in the present moment in a manner that is more important than the past or the future. The focus, in much of the preaching of Jesus, is on the present as a privileged time *(kairos),* challenging his hearers to accept that their experience of the here and now is an experience of grace. This proclamation by Jesus that the Reign of God is at hand, continued by the Church, is as valid today in the twentieth century with the same immediacy as it was in the first century.

A third element summarising the proclamation of Jesus is the call 'to repent and to believe in the gospel'. There is a clear logic at work here. If the goal of history is really close by, then this means that the Reign of God is about to take place; and if the Reign of God is imminent, then those who are present for this great event in the history of Israel will have to get ready through a process of repentance and conversion to the demands of the Kingdom.

These three elements, the right time *(kairos),* the nearness of the Reign of God, and the call to repentance are at the heart of the gospel of Christ. The whole life of Jesus was taken up with presenting one or other of these aspects of the gospel. All the words and deeds of Jesus can be seen as a testimony to the coming of God's Reign into our world. For instance, most of the parables and the sayings of Jesus are about the meaning and content of the Kingdom. In a similar manner many of the miracles and much of the behaviour of Jesus are symbolic of the change and transformation that the advent of the Kingdom of God will effect.

In spite of the extensive data on the Reign of God in the gospels, it is extremely difficult to grasp the full range of meaning attached to this powerful and evocative symbol. Some consolation as well as instruction should be taken from the fact that Jesus never defined the Reign of God as such. Instead he preferred to talk about it in different symbolic stories. A similar diversity can be found in the variety of activity mediating the presence of the Reign of God in our midst: caring for the poor, feeding the hungry, healings, exorcisms, prophetic acts of forgiveness and symbolic gestures of reconciliation. Acknowledging these difficulties, none the less we need to be able to make some preliminary statement about the meaning of the Reign of God, no matter how inadequate and incomplete it may be, before turning to the implications of the parables and the miracles.

It is evident in the teaching of Jesus that the coming of the Reign of God into our world is an offer of grace and new life from God; in this way, the Reign of God is something that begins and ends with God. The eschatological aspect of this multi-layered symbol ensures that it cannot be exhausted by the images and expectations which arise from human experience; it is transcendent in origin and in destiny, and thus cannot be brought into being simply and solely by human efforts. The Reign of God announced by Jesus to some extent represents a radical discontinuity with the limitations of a world which has been tainted with sin and death, as much of the biblical language concerned with the eschaton insists on conveying (e.g. Mk 13:24-27; 1 Co 15:42-44; 1 Jn 3:2; Rv 21:1).

Paradoxically, the Reign of God also contains a profound continuity with present human experience. This is evident in the facility with which Jesus draws diverse images from the world of his audience's experience in order to illustrate aspects of the Kingdom (as will be examined below); even more importantly, the profound continuity is evident in the invitational aspect of the symbol – in Jesus' call for a human response to the Reign of God which includes the joint cooperation of people with the plan of God for the world. In other words, the future Reign of God is about the gathering up by God into a condition of fulfilment and transformation of all the human efforts in this life which are directed towards the creation of peace and justice in the world around us. The Reign of God is about God and humanity flourishing together in a new relationship; the Reign of God is about God enabling the human enterprise to realise its full potential as well as that which lies beyond a purely human potential; the Reign of God is ultimately about re-establishing right relationships between God and humanity, between humanity and the individual, between humanity and the whole of creation.

Without neglecting the essential eschatological aspect of this multi-layered symbol, and to some extent because of this aspect, it must be asserted that the Reign of God is a theological symbol which carries with it profound social and ecological implications. The Reign of God cannot be treated as if it pertained only to certain aspects of reality, which might be conceived of as solely 'spiritual', 'other-worldly' and 'transcendent'. The Kingdom is rather concerned with all of human life reaching a level of fruition which will ultimately be brought to full term by the transforming action of God. While the Kingdom does not originate in this world and while it cannot be limited by this world it does, none the less, touch the conditions of this world in a concrete and tangible manner. The eschatological aspect of the Kingdom-symbol stresses that the Kingdom comes from God and that only God can bring the initiative made in the person of Jesus to fulfilment; the invitational aspect of the symbol, however, is addressed to individuals and calls forth a response from the communty in the historical here and now.

The preaching of Jesus in the gospels reveals this tension in the Kingdom symbol when it proclaims the Reign of God both as something offered in the present and promised as future gift. This tension between the present and the future has given rise to two different interpretations of the Kingdom. Some say the Reign of God has already come in the ministry of Jesus and so they talk about the presence of a realised eschatology in the New Testament, especially in the Gospel of John (C.H. Dodd). Others claim that Jesus expected the Reign of God to come in his own lifetime and so they refer to the existence of a futuristic eschatology in the preaching of Jesus. Some mediating position must be found to keep these two points of view together.

There can be no doubt that Jesus refers to the Kingdom as present on several occasions. The Kingdom, says Jesus, 'is at hand' (Mk 1:15) and 'is in the midst of you' (Lk 17:21). Care must be exercised here concerning the way we interpret these sayings of Jesus. The expression 'is at hand' is linguistically ambiguous. It can mean the Kingdom has already come, or it can mean that the Kingdom is coming, is close by, is drawing near. The latter interpretation, highlighted by J. Weiss and A. Schweitzer, is the more accepted one.[6] But what then are we to make of statements like 'but if it is by the spirit of God that I cast out demons, then the Kingdom of God has come upon you' (Mt 12:28; Lk 11:20). Verses like these and others seem to be saying that the Kingdom is present in embryo when certain things take place and that these moments are fragmentary glimpses of what is to come in the future. It is only in virtue of these concrete intimations of the Kingdom in the present that Jesus can talk about the future realisation of the Kingdom. Indeed, Jesus highlights these fragmentary glimpses of the Kingdom when he is asked by the disciples of John the Baptist 'Are you he who is to come or shall we look for another?'. And Jesus replied:

> Go and tell John what you hear and see: the blind receive their sight and the lame walk, lepers are cleansed and the deaf hear, and the dead are raised up and the poor have the good news preached to them (Mt 11:3-5).

It is these mediating activities in the present that provide glimpses of what is to come in the future and at the same time give credibility to Jesus' prayer and promise about the Kingdom in the future:

> Thy Kingdom come
> Thy will be done
> On earth as it is in heaven (Mt 6:10).

What is significant here, indeed normative, both in the life of Jesus and in the Church today is that we can only talk meaningfully about the future event of the Kingdom in so far as there are in present existence some tangible anticipations and symbolic intimations of what is to come. To be sure, the thrust of some of Jesus' preaching and praxis is futuristic, but this is so only in the light of what is taking place in the present ministry of Jesus: healing, exorcisms, forgiveness of sins, care of the poor and the initiation of a new table fellowship for all. There appears to be a strong emphasis throughout the ministry of Jesus on the importance of certain liberating actions as symbolic mediations providing a foretaste in the present of the

6   See B.T. Viviano, *The Kingdom of God in History*, op. cit. pp. 15-16.

Kingdom to come. What are these liberating activities? They would include bringing good news to the poor, feeding the hungry, freeing the oppressed, healing the sick, offering unconditional forgiveness to sinners, and the setting up of a new kind of open table fellowship. These activities are indicative, if not normative, of the kind of activities that christians today should be involved in for the sake of the coming Reign of God. Only in this way will we be able to talk meaningfully and credibly about the existence of a creative tension between the present and the future as one of the hallmarks of christian existence. What is important is that our language describing the Kingdom both in the ministry of Jesus and in the life of the Church should be marked by reference to this tension, this creative tension, between the present and the future.

The Parables and Miracles of Jesus

Perhaps the best clue to the meaning of the Kingdom is given to us in the parables of Jesus. Most would agree that the parables represent the authentic teaching of Jesus on the Kingdom, even though this teaching has been worked over in many instances by the post-paschal community. What is instructive about the parables is that they present Jesus' own perception of the coming Reign of God. As such, the parables express symbolically the vision and content of the Kingdom of God. In doing so, the parables describe in many instances the spiritual and social transformation that the Reign of God brings about in the world as present experience and future promise.

What is striking about the parables as a literary genre is that they often call into question the accepted structures of reality: they shatter our conventional way of experiencing and understanding the world, they startle the individual out of complacency, they open up 'the possibility of a new and different kind of living'[7] in the present, they 'tease the mind into new perceptions of reality'[8] Most of all, as we shall presently see, they give rise to a liberating praxis that

7   E. Schillebeeckx, *Jesus, An Experiment in Christology*, London: Collins, 1979, p. 169.
8   N. Perrin, *Jesus and the Language of the Kingdom*, op. cit. p. 106.

issues in a new way of experiencing God in the world.

One of the great difficulties in approaching the parables about the Reign of God is the wide range of parables in the gospels. At first glance each parable seems to have its own particular perspective on the Kingdom. Is there any overall pattern to this diversity of parables? Many different ways of classifying the parables have been suggested: narrative, metaphor, insight.[9] One particularly helpful proposal has been put forward by John D. Crossan. He suggests a basic framework within which most of the parables can be situated. This framework is based on two parables in Matthew's gospel and one parable in the apocryphal gospel of Thomas. The parables in question are the hidden treasure, the pearl of great price (Mt 13:44-46) and the great fish (gospel of Thomas 81:28-82:3). These particular parables contain a threefold pattern which sums up the overall framework of most of the other parables and the underlying experience of the coming Reign of God. The underlying perspective is one of advent, reversal, and action.[10] For example, in the parable of the hidden treasure the sudden and unexpected advent of the treasure takes the individual by surprise. This discovery brings about a dramatic change and reversal in lifestyle: he sells 'all that he has'. This decision, in turn, leads to the action of buying the field. Everything flows from the advent-experience of discovering the treasure in the field. So it is with the Reign of God. There is the discovery, more specifically the co-experience, of the gracious presence of God as King in history and Lord of creation. This disarming co-presence of God brings about a significant change in perspective and this issues in a new kind of living.

According to Crossan this threefold structure of advent-reversal-action runs through most of the parables in one form or another. In some parables the element of discovery and advent are to the fore, such as the parables of the fig tree, the lost sheep, and the lost coin. In other parables the focus is on change and renewal, such as the parables about the pharisee and the publican, the rich man and

---

9   See B.B. Scott, *Jesus, Symbol Maker for the Kingdom*, Philadelphia: Fortress Press, 1981.
10   J.D. Crossan, *In Parables: The Challenge of the Historical Jesus*, New York: Harper & Row, 1973, pp.35-36.

Lazarus, and the prodigal son. Thirdly, there are parables in which the emphasis is on a new kind of action/praxis such as the parables about the talents, the wicked husband-men, and the unmerciful servant.

The general validity of this approach to the parables on the Kingdom is borne out by its coherence with the rest of the teaching of Jesus on the Kingdom which also emphasises one or other aspect of this threefold pattern of advent-reversal-action (e.g. Mk 8:35, 10:15, 10:31; Mt 5:39ff; Lk 9:60-62). In particular, the pattern of advent-reversal-action corresponds most closely with the demand for conversion that accompanies contact with the Kingdom of God (cf. Mk 1:15; Jn 3:3). A brief note on each one of these three dimensions will help to capture the significance of the Reign of God in the mission and ministry of Jesus.

Advent: The primary thrust of the mission of Jesus is to point up the advent, the coming of the Reign of God into our world. The Reign of God is coming with a new urgency in the preaching and praxis of Jesus; God is now personally active as King in the person of Jesus. The advent of the Reign of God is pure gift, an offer of new life from God which makes demands, confers a task, and effects change in the lives of those who have ears to hear and eyes to see. This gracious coming of the Reign of God in the person of Jesus is mediated not so much by extraordinary signs (Lk 17:20-21) but in the more ordinary experiences of bringing good news to the poor, release to captives, sight to the blind, and freedom to those who are oppressed (Lk 4:18). The nearness of the Reign of God is co-experienced in those activities that advance the human condition in the world. One of the predominating concerns of the liberating activity of Jesus associated with the coming Reign of God in the world is the well-being of all members of the human family with an evident priority for the poor. The Kingship of God is manifested as gift whenever and wherever individuals are moved from the margins of existence to the centre of life.

Reversal: This coming of the Reign of God brings about a reversal of the values of this world. The world begins to look different and takes on a different complexion in the light of the imminent Reign of God. A change of heart and a new set of priorities begins to emerge. The spirit of this reversal is best summed up in terms of the Beatitudes. In the presence of the Reign of God it is the poor in spirit that are rich, the peace-makers are called sons and daughters of God, the humbled are exalted, those who mourn are blessed (Mt 5:3ff). Likewise, love is shown not only to your friends but also to your enemies, when you are asked to go one mile you must be prepared to go two miles, to enter the Kingdom you must become like little children, and only those who lose their lives for the sake of the Kingdom will save their lives (see Mt 10:39; Mt 19:14). An index of the radical character of this reversal of values can be gauged by the following words of Jesus:

> You know that rulers of the Gentiles lord it over them, and their great men exercise authority over them. It shall not be so among you; but whoever would be great among you must be your servant and whoever would be first among you must be your slave (Mt 20:25-26).

Encounter with the grace of the coming of the Reign of God carries with it this radical turning upside down (Ac 17:6) of the values of this world. An essential element in this reversal is the challenge to a new kind of living which brings us to the third element of the experience of the coming Reign of God.

Action: One of the outstanding features of the preaching of Jesus on the Kingdom of God is the consistent emphasis that is placed on praxis both in the parables and in the rest of his teaching. This focus on praxis arises out of the urgency accompanying the present advent of the Reign of God. Crossan is not alone in detecting this emphasis on praxis in the parables. Amos Wilder points out:

> In the parables we have action images ... Jesus' speech had the character ... of compelling imagination ... and transformation.[11]

What is equally significant about the parables of Jesus in this context is that they rarely present us merely with a theory about the

---

11 A. Wilder, *Early Christian Rhetoric: The Language of the Gospel*, New York: Harvard University Press, 1971, p. 84.

Kingdom. Rather, the parables provide us with a symbolic vision of the Reign of God that calls forth an immediate response of praxis. The praxis demanded by the parables is not some kind of mechanical or mindless activity. Instead it is a creative and imaginative praxis inspired by the co-experience of the nearness of the Reign of God and the promise this co-presence embodies for the future. The praxis in question therefore is directed towards a transformation of the historical situation of individuals and the existing structures within society. In other words, the proclamation by Jesus of the Reign of God is not to be understood primarily in terms of providing propositional information about some external reality out there. Rather it is a proclamation that contains an interactive power and force in relation to the way society is organised and structured. It is this interpretative force and power in the proclamation of Jesus that generates a liberating praxis in the life of Jesus and among his disciples.[12]

A good example of this unity between the vision and praxis of the Kingdom can be found in the parable of the talents (Mt 25:14-30). The enterprising praxis of the servants with the five talents and the three talents is a matter of praise by the master, whereas the paralysing inactivity of the servant with one talent is the object of rejection. The mere maintenance of the status quo by the servant with the one talent is condemned as being out of joint with the urgent demands of the coming Reign of God. A lack of trust in the potential and promise of life, as well as an overly cautious approach, in the life of the servant with one talent, is condemned. One commentator aptly sums up the parable:

> Moreover his (the servant with one talent) verbal expression of fear and his refusal to risk action are an implicit accusation against life itself. They showed he viewed the universe as inimical to the human enterprise and saw self defensive non-action, therefore, as the appropriate course to take in life.[13]

---

12 F.S. Fiorenza, *Foundational Theology: Jesus and the Church*, New York: pp. 116-118.
13 D.O. Via, *The Parables*, Philadelphia: Fortress Press, 1967, p. 119. What is significant about this emphasis on action in the parables is that it was picked up by Via, Wilder and Crossan at a time when little attention was given to the importance of praxis in the gospels.

In contrast, the thrust of the parables is by and large towards the kind of activity that brings about change and transformation in the world. The individual who hears the words of Jesus (vision) and does them (praxis) is compared to a person who built a house upon a rock, whereas the individual who hears the words of Jesus and does not do them is like a person who built a house on sand (Mt 7:24-27). The classic example of this praxis orientation in the preaching of Jesus is to be found in the story about the final judgment:

> The king will say ... Come ... inherit the kingdom, I was hungry and you gave me food ... as you did it to one of the least you did it to me (Mt 25:31ff).

The strongest argument for this unity between vision and praxis is the personal life-style of Jesus. The preaching of Jesus on the Kingdom is consistently matched by a liberating praxis towards those who were oppressed in Palestinian society. Jesus, we are told, 'went about doing good': healing the sick, performing exorcisms, forgiving sins, and entering into a new kind of table fellowship with those who were outcast. Each of these activities brings about a change in the social situation of the individual in Palestine. This liberating praxis of Jesus is important, indeed is primary, because it is held up as symbolic of the coming Reign of God (Mt 12:28, Lk 10:9, Mt 11:4ff). Further, this praxis of Jesus, which is inspired by his conviction of the coming Reign of God, is always of the type that gives rise to the liberation of the individual in the here and now. It is this freeing of persons in the present that predominates in the praxis of Jesus and as such is taken as symbolic of the future. The basic orientation arising out of the vision of the Kingdom of God is more than simply one of giving importance to action; it is about according primary significance to a liberating praxis in the light of the reigning co-presence of God.

James P. Mackey sums up Jesus' understanding of the Reign of God in terms quite similar to those of advent-reversal-action. According to Mackey, 'the essence of the Kingdom of God lies in the activity of relating to things as precious, as gift or grace already there'.[14] The Reign of God is about discovering 'relations of grace'[15] in life and this involves a recognition of things and people as gift or grace in contrast to that attitude which simply approaches things and people in terms of a selfish grasping. These relationships of grace, therefore, revise totally all that this world has ever expected of kings and lords: a leadership of service, the offer of unconditional forgiveness, an open table fellowship, and a new inclusive belongingness of all to God. For Mackey it is this vision of existence as a relationship of grace that generates a healing and transformative practice in the lives of people.[16]

These relations of grace that characterise the Reign of God must be understood also to include humanity's relationship to the earth. In the Hebrew scriptures, the people's relationship with Yahweh included a relationship with the whole of creation, especially the land, and this motif is part of the preaching of Jesus. The earth and its fruit is available not for a relationship of domination and manipulation but as part of a relationship of grace that offers life. The exclusion of the earth from relations of grace is in part an eclipse of the full Reign of God in our world. It is surely no accident that many of the parables of Jesus invoke agricultural images from the earth to describe the dynamics of the Reign of God in our world: the mustard seed, the leaven, and the vineyard. There is more than a hint in the parables of Jesus that the earth and its cycle of life is an important key to a proper understanding of the present and future Reign of God.

What is equally revelatory about the Reign of God and the place of praxis within this proclamation is the prominence of the miracles in the mission of Jesus. Many of the miracles of Jesus are presented as signs of the coming Reign of God:

> But if it is by the finger of God that I cast out demons, then the Kingdom of God has come upon you (Mt 12:28).

The miracles are symbolic anticipations and intimations of what

14 James P. Mackey, *Modern Theology: A Sense of Direction*, Oxford: Oxford University Press, 1987, p. 113.
15 J.P. Mackey, op.cit. pp. 113-115, and 119.
16 J.P. Mackey, op.cit. p. 115.

the final coming Reign of God will effect in the lives of people, namely healing and holiness, liberation and reconciliation, a new unity and integration of life.

An exaggerated emphasis on the miracles of Jesus in the past as well as a more empirical awareness today of the relationship between cause and effect has given rise to scepticism among some people today. For example, a presentation of the miracles as proofs of the divinity of Jesus misses the mark and loses sight of their original context. Equally, a purely literal approach can distort their meaning and diminishes the challenge they present for the christian community today. Further, any suggestion that the miracles are simply a kind of manipulation of nature is theologically un-productive in the long run because it seems to imply among other things that nature prior to the miracles is somehow devoid of a divine presence – a point of view that is contrary to the Reigning Lordship of Yahweh in history and in creation already discussed above.

While it is true to say that many of the miracles reflect a post-Easter interest from the early Church, this does not mean that they can be dismissed simply as ecclesial creations. Instead, what the miracles of Jesus symbolise is that the Reign of God coming into the world brings about a new kind of harmony between God and humanity, between the individual and the community, between the community and the earth, that is both transformative and re-demptive in its effects. Whenever God and humanity draw closely together, whenever the community respects the primacy of the individual, and whenever humanity reveres the life of nature, then truly extraordinary things begin to happen in the world around us like healing, forgiveness and communion. This coming together of God and humanity, this special regard for the individual within the community, this respect for the harmony of life between humans and the earth took place in the ministry of Jesus and can take place today in the christian community with equally extraordinary results.

When we put together the parables and the miracles of Jesus we begin to glimpse some of the richness contained in the coming Reign of God and begin to see some of the plan of God for the world revealed in the words and deeds of Jesus; we see what can happen in the present when the co-presence of God as King and Lord is acknowledged and accepted in praxis. Something of a 'revolution' begins to take place in the lives of people and in their relationship with nature when God is allowed to reign. Above all the demands of the present moment take on a new significance and urgency in virtue of the preaching and praxis of Jesus. In theological terms we can conclude that the proclamation of Jesus in relation to the Reign of God unites the horizontal and the vertical aspects of God's co-presence in creation and history, a thesis that we will take up in the next chapter.

2

Theological Reflections on the Reign of God

Our biblical introduction to the Reign of God in the life of Jesus leaves many questions unanswered. These include issues like what was the source of Jesus' insight into the Reign of God, how are we to interpret the revelation of God as Father, and what is the relationship between praxis and the coming Reign of God? The purpose of this chapter is to provide some preliminary theological responses to these questions.

A Vision Rooted in Jesus' Experience of God

Where did Jesus get his insights into the Reign and Realm of God? Is it enough to suggest that he inherited them from the Hebrew scriptures and the religious traditions of first-century Palestine?

To be sure, the traditions of Israel do play a foundational role in the preaching and praxis of Jesus. However, we suggest that there was an additional factor animating the Kingdom vision and praxis of Jesus. This other factor can be summed up in terms of his profound awareness of and personal relationship with God. More specifically we propose that it was Jesus' personal experience of God that ultimately shaped and influenced his vision and praxis of the coming Reign of God. In particular, we hold along with other contemporary christologists that it was Jesus' personal encounter with God as Father that was the driving force of his whole mission and ministry.[1] A close connection exists between Jesus' procla-

1   E. Schillebeeckx, *Jesus: An Experiment in Christology*, London: Collins, 1979, p. 257ff. W.M. Thompson, *Jesus Debate: A Survey and Synthesis*, New York: Paulist Press, 1985, pp. 185-186.

mation of the coming Reign of God and his personal experience of God as Father. To appreciate this connection we need to attend to Jesus's personal relationship with God and this in turn requires looking at some of the factors that influenced the experience of this relationship.

The religious experience of Jesus is shaped by his Jewish background. As we have already seen in chapter 1 this background, from a theological point of view, focuses on the liberating action of God in history (Exodus, Covenant, Exile and Return) and the sustaining power of God in creation. Within this double context, God is presented in a variety of different ways: king, judge, lord, rock, father, mother (Nb 11:12, Dt 32:18, Is 49:15, 66:13).

Another factor shaping the human and religious experience of Jesus would have been his parents, Mary and Joseph. There can be little doubt that the special circumstances surrounding the birth of Jesus would have had a bearing on Jesus' subsequent experience of God as Father. Mary's special relationship with Jesus during his childhood as well as the unique situation obtaining between Jesus as son and Joseph as foster father would each in their own way have been elements affecting the religious development and education of Jesus. It is hardly a flight of fancy to surmise that Jesus' experience of family, especially in terms of his special relationships with Mary and Joseph, his experience of prayer, and his observance of Jewish religious duties would have influenced his subsequent experience and understanding of God as *Abba*.

Given these background influences we can now look at Jesus' personal experience of God as Father and its particular connection with the coming Reign of God. Recent scripture studies have highlighted the centrality of God as Father in the ministry of Jesus and have suggested that the personal address of God as Father/*Abba*, especially in prayer, was an important part of the uniqueness of Jesus. The expression and articulation of Jesus' experience of God in terms of Father is quite clear from the New Testament evidence. God is referred to as Father some 170 times in the gospels: four times in Mark, fifteen in Luke, forty-two in Matthew and 109 in John. This New Testament usage exists in sharp contrast to the Hebrew scriptures which refer explicitly to God as Father in only nineteen places, and only three of these references address God.[2]

By far the most influential name associated with the presentation of Jesus' understanding of God as Father/*Abba* is Joachim Jeremias.[3] According to Jeremias, the New Testament references to God are inspired ultimately by Jesus' personal address of God in prayer as *Abba*. The retention of the Aramaic word *Abba* in the New Testament in Mark 14:36, Romans 8:15 and Galatians 4:6 is regarded by Jeremias as most significant and decisive. It suggests that the New Testament references to God as Father, 'my Father' and 'our Father' all go back to Jesus' use of *Abba*. Further, for Jeremias, when Jesus used the Aramaic term *Abba* he was deliberately using the language of a child and as such intended to communicate a sense of intimacy and informality with God. *Abba*, implies Jeremias, is more properly translated as the informal 'Daddy', in contrast to 'Father'.

Jeremias' work has been influential in christological circles and has gained widespread acceptance. Recent studies, however, have begun to challenge Jeremias' interpretation of the evidence. James Barr, for example, questions on semantic grounds the claim that the proper translation of the word *Abba* is 'Daddy' rather than the adult term 'Father'.[4] Further, Barr wonders whether the different references to God as Father, 'my Father' and 'our Father', can be traced back to the single semitic form of *Abba*. He 'suggests (a) the probability of a form that specifies "our" Father rather than the indeterminate *Abba*, and (b) the likelihood that Jesus himself might have used this form, either in the Hebrew or in the Aramaic'.[5] At the same time, however, Barr concludes:

2   See 2 S 7:14; 1 Ch 17:13; 1 Ch 22:10; 1 Ch 28:6; Ps 89:27 which describe in general terms the relationship that will obtain between God and the King in the period of the monarchy. See also Ps 103:13; Dt 32:6; Dt 32:18; Jr 3:4-5; Jr 31:9; Is 63:16; Ml 1:6; Tb 13:4; Ws 2:16; 11:10; 14:3; Si 23:1; 23:4; 51:10 which talk about God in the broad context of Israel, sin, repentance and forgiveness. Si 23:1; Si 1:4; and Ws 14:3 are addressed to God.
3   See *The Prayers of Jesus*, London: SCM Press, 1967; New Testament Theology, London: SCM Press, 1971.
4   J. Barr, '*Abba* Isn't Daddy'. *Journal of Theological Studies* 39 (1988) 28-47; '*Abba*, Father'. *Theology* XCI (1988) 173-179.
5   '*Abba* isn't Daddy', *Journal of Theological Studies* 39 (1988) 44.

The importance of the fatherhood of God for Jesus is amply evidenced in many places and is not in question here; the only question is the degree of its connection with the sole term 'Abba', and in the nuance that is imparted through that connection.[6]

Approaching the same question from a slightly different point of view, some feminist scholars have also begun to re-assess the New Testament evidence concerning references to God as Father.[7] In general terms they point out that as a matter of fact the word *Abba*, in contrast to Father, is attributed to Jesus only once, namely in the prayer scene in Gethsemane and that then there were no witnesses since Jesus was alone (Mk 14:36). Further, it is also noted that references to God as Father are relatively few in the earlier documents and that they become much more frequent in later documents of the New Testament. For example, in Mark there are only four references to God as Father whereas in John there are 109. In particular, feminist scholars are concerned to show that Jesus did talk about God in images other than the image of Father and that these images such as God as a baker woman or a woman householder are equally important in coming to an understanding of the mystery of God. Feminist scholars make the important point that the thrust of Jesus' understanding of God, whether male or female, cannot be taken as a justification of patriarchy.[8]

These recent studies demand at least that we be more circumspect in the way we interpret Jesus' experience of God. They forewarn us against making claims that go beyond the evidence or reading into the text meanings that might be interpreted in exclusively androcentric terms. These studies, however, do not diminish the importance of Jesus' experience of God, nor do they detract from his expression of this experience in terms of God as Father and the

6   '*Abba,* Father', *Theology* XCI (1988), 179.
7   M. Boucher, 'Scriptural Readings: God Language and Non Sexist Translations' in B.A. Withers (ed.) *Language and the Church*, New York: National Council of Churches of Christ in the USA, 1984; M. Collins, 'Naming God in Public Prayer' originally published in *Worship* 59 (1985) 291-304 and now available in *Worship, Renewal to Practice*, Washington DC: The Pastoral Press, 1987, pp. 215-229.
8   A. Carr, 'Feminist Reflections on God', *Transforming Grace*, New York: Harper and Row, 1988 p. 147.

relationship of this to the proclamation of the coming Reign of God.

What is significant about the New Testament evidence is that when Jesus talks about God, he rarely talks about God *per se*. Instead, Jesus talks in most instances about God as Father or about the Reign of God. The proclamations of God as Father and the Reign of God are proclamations about a God who is *radically relational*. The announcement of God as Father is spelt out socially in terms of the Reign of God and the proclamation of the Reign of God is grounded in Jesus' experience of God as Father. Further, when Jesus does talk about God as Father and the Reign of God, he does so in a way that transcends any traces of patriarchy and repudiates all forms of power-seeking domination.

This transcending of patriarchy by Jesus, especially through his perception of God as Father, is an important element in his teaching. Paradoxically, the transformation of patriarchy in the New Testament is rooted in Jesus' experience of God as Father. This can be seen by contrasting Jesus' experience and understanding of God as Father with the religious experience and understanding of some of the ancient religions. Further, the repudiation of patriarchy is evident in the new community of equals that Jesus establishes in his ministry.

Within the history of many of the ancient world religions we find the presence of a primordial experience that perceives humanity as the offspring of the gods. Ancient peoples, such as the Egyptians, Assyrians, Greeks and Romans often understood themselves as somehow naturally begotten by the deity or deities. As a result the divinity was often invoked in terms of Father and this in turn is related to some extent to the origins of patriarchy with its focus on concepts such as *paterfamilias* (father of the household) and *patris potestas* (power of the father) which have become so problematic today.

This primitive experience describing a genealogical relationship between God/gods and humanity is transformed by Jesus. Jesus picks up this ancient experience and gives it a radically new shape in terms of his personal relationship with God as Father. What is important here is that Jesus does not associate the God of his experience with these primitive myths of divine generation or natural descent from the deity, nor does Jesus endorse the cultural assumptions underlying these myths. Instead, the God of Jesus is the God of Abraham and Sarah, that is a God of election and vocation, a God who chooses the people of Israel as God's own people in and through a historical process: 'Israel is my first born son' (Ex 4:22; see also Ho 11:1; Jr 31:9). It is this divine election of Israel by Yahweh that lies behind the notion of God as Father in the Hebrew scriptures. 'Is he (i.e. Yahweh) not your father who formed you? Did he not make you and establish you?' (Dt 32:6). Thus contrary to popular perception the God of the Hebrew scriptures does not endorse the ancient myths of procreation by the deity, nor does the God of Israel support the cultural suppositions of patriarchy lying behind these myths.[9]

It is this historical experience of Israel that Jesus affirms and deepens in his own personal experience of God as Father. In other words, a number of revelatory moves are concentrated and condensed in Jesus' non-patriarchal experience of God as Father. These moves are perhaps best understood as evocative of Israel's historical experience rather than pure innovation on the part of Jesus. Jesus' experience of God as Father sums up and personifies in a special way Israel's corporate experience of Yahweh. Israel's historical experience of Yahweh in turn both resonates with and at the same time must be distinguished from the primitive experience of ancient peoples who understood themselves as somehow the natural offspring of patriarchal divinities. In effect the personal experience of God by Jesus therefore should not be presented as an isolated religious experience. Instead it is a religious experience that has historical roots reaching deep down into Israel's religious experience and beyond Israel into the archaeology of ancient religions respectively. The experience of Jesus is the purification and culmination of humanity's innermost orientation towards God from the dawn of time.

---

9 See W. Kasper, *The God of Jesus Christ*, London: Burns and Oates, 1984, pp. 138-139; S. Schneider, *Women and the Word*, New York: Paulist Press, 1986, pp. 28-37; C. Geffré, *The Risk of Interpretation*, New York: Paulist Press, 1987, pp. 130-131. A possible exception to this generalisation may be found in Dt 32:8; Ps 29:1; Ps 89:7.

The other factor in the ministry of Jesus which transcends patriarchy is his calling into being of a new community of a discipleship of equals. The setting up by Jesus of a new alternative community of women and men is closely connected to his experience of God as Father. Because there is one God who is Father of all, a new set of non-patriarchal relationships is introduced among those who acknowledge God as Father through their discipleship of Jesus. This new relationship among women and men transcends natural ties and as such is a direct consequence of Jesus' proclamation of the fatherhood of God. Indeed, when women and men relate to each other as sister and brother in virtue of this universal fatherhood of God, then the Reign of God is coming into being:

> Looking around on those who sat about him, he said 'here are my mother and my brother. Whoever does the will of God is my brother, and sister, and mother' (Mk 3:34-35).

One of the distinctive qualities therefore of the coming Reign of God announced by Jesus and inspired by his experience of God is this inclusive discipleship between young and old, rich and poor, insider and outsider, male and female. All are called without distinction to belong to the one inclusive/non-patriarchal family of God the Father. Thus Jesus can say to the disciples who make up this new alternative community of equals:

> And call no man your father on earth, for you have one Father who is in heaven (Mt 23:9).

We can only become part of the kingdom when we live according to this vision of radical equality among all disciples in a relationship open to all members of the human race. The source and origin of this new vision of women and men as sisters and brothers living and working together under the Reign of God is Jesus' experience of God as Father.

It is this extraordinary experience of Jesus that constitutes the foundation of his understanding of the coming Reign of God. An intrinsic connection exists between Jesus' experience of God as Father and his vision of the coming Reign of God. This connection is perhaps best appreciated by attending to the theological implications of Jesus' experience of God as Father. These implications can be summed up under two interrelated headings which capture some of the essential features of the coming Reign of God: the fatherhood of God and the unique sonship of Jesus.

It is in virtue of his experience of God as Father that Jesus proclaims the coming Reign of God. He is able to talk about 'my Father' and 'your Father' in his discussions with his disciples (Mt 5:45, 6:1, 7:11; 18:35; Lk 12:32). He prays 'our Father', and talks freely about 'the Father' who loves, forgives and receives all with open arms. The God announced in the coming Reign of God is a provident and caring God who is Father of all, who 'makes the sun rise on the evil and on the good, and sends the rain on the just and the unjust' (Mt 5:45), and who, at the same time, is solicitous for all including the birds of the air and the lilies of the field (Mt 6:26, 32).

Within this experience and understanding of the fatherhood of God by Jesus there is a strong sense of his Sonship. Indeed, one of the most basic and consistent themes running through the gospel story is the unique Sonship of Jesus. One finds this theme of Sonship in varying degrees of explicitness throughout the life of Jesus. Some would argue that it is present implicitly in the finding of the child in the temple which alludes to the Sonship of Jesus by referring to his heavenly Father, though it must be admitted that this incident bears more the marks of later theological reflection by the early Church than that of historical record. This is followed by the theophany at the baptism in the Jordan: 'Thou art my beloved Son, with thee I am well pleased' (Lk 3:22). This in turn is re-echoed in the complex incident of the Transfiguration which is both messianic and Son-centred. The same theme becomes more explicit in the Garden of Gethsemane when Jesus prays '*Abba*, Father, all things are possible to thee; remove this cup from me' (Mk 14:36). Lastly, there are the final words of Jesus on the cross: 'Father, into your hands I commend my spirit' (Lk 23:46). While it is true that these reports reflect the influence of the post-Easter Church they do capture the unfolding historical relationship that exists between Jesus as Son and God as Father.

The underlying relationship between Jesus as Son and God as Father takes on the character of a revelation of God in a manner analogous to the way a human son represents/reveals his earthly father. The dynamic unity between Jesus the Son and God the Father is summed up in the saying: 'All things have been delivered to me by my Father; no one knows the Son except the Father and no one knows the Father except the Son and anyone to whom the Son chooses to reveal him' (Mt 11:27). It is in the theologically developed Johannine writings that this special relationship between the Son and the Father is most explicitly developed. In the writings of John, Jesus is referred to as 'the Son of God' (Jn 20:31; 1 Jn 5:20). For John, the Father and the Son are one (Jn 10:30, 17:11, 21-23); their words and deeds inhere in each other (Jn 14:10, 11, 20; 17:21-23). Thus it can be said that there is Fatherhood because there is Sonship and equally there is Sonship because there is Fatherhood. Perhaps nowhere is it clearer that we cannot fully understand Jesus simply from below because Jesus understands himself from above, as Kasper rightly reminds us.[10]

The Language of God as Father

It should be more than clear at this stage that Jesus' experience of God as Father is crucial both for an understanding of his proclamation of the Reign of God and for the development of this proclamation into a systematic christology. Yet at the same time it must be acknowledged that the language of God as Father, Jesus as Son and the Kingdom of God is increasingly problematic at a theoretical and practical level for at least half of the human race. The women's movement both within the Church and outside the christian community is critical of any language that is predominantly or exclusively male. It is argued with rigour by both christian and non-christian feminists that language influences the way we see the world and shapes the way we experience reality. For many, language 'houses' reality. Further, it is noted by many christians today that the persistent use of only one particular language in the life and worship of the Church can give rise to sexism and tends to

10 W. Kasper, *Jesus the Christ*, London: Burns & Oates, 1976, p. 248.

legitimate the existence of patriarchy within the christian community. In addition, it is suggested that the present unnuanced use of theological language in the Church is causing considerable alienation and anger among women from a pastoral, liturgical and spiritual point of view.

A number of serious and searching questions arise at this juncture that are simply unavoidable today in the light of the Women's Movement.[11] Is the revelation of God as Father by Jesus something that must be taken literally and therefore interpreted as somehow justifying the legitimacy of patriarchy? Is the mystery of God wrapped up exclusively in the use of masculine images and language? Is christianity a religion primarily of fathers and sons and therefore patriarchal in foundation? Is God male?

An adequate answer to these complex questions exceeds the purpose of this chapter. At most, we can only describe, in broad strokes, the direction such an answer might take. In the first place recourse must be had to the doctrine of the radical incomprehensibility of God.[12] Before and in the presence of the mystery of God there is no fully adequate image, picture, or theory. Even the revelation of God in Jesus, which ultimately issues in the doctrine of the Blessed Trinity, is subject to a recognition of the incomprehensibility of God, that is, the God revealed in Jesus continues to be the God who 'dwells in light unapproachable' (1 Tm 6:16) and 'whose judgments are unsearchable and ways inscrutable' (Rm 11:33). Thus we find Augustine pointing out that if you have understood, then what you have understood is not God: *si comprehenderis, non est Deus*. Similarly, Aquinas states that the one thing we know about God is that we do not know God. At most, we can arrive at the advanced state of what some call 'learned ignorance' *(docta ignorantia)* and others refer to as a condition of 'knowing the unknown'.

The doctrine of analogy, developed by Aquinas, is intended to safeguard and protect the incomprehensible mystery of God. In

11 See A. Carr, *Transforming Grace*, op. cit. ch. 7.
12 This particular issue is treated with admirable care and clarity by E. Johnson, 'The Incomprehensibility of God and the Image of God Male and Female' *Theological Studies* 45 (1984), 441-465.

brief, the doctrine of analogy reminds us that every 'is' statement about God must be followed by an even more important 'is not' statement. The way of affirmation in theology is followed by the way of negation, and this in turn gives rise to the way of eminence (refinement). In this regard we do well to recall that according to the fourth Lateran Council (1215) the realm of dissimilarity (is not) is greater than the realm of similarity (is) in our discourse about God.

In the context of the particular questions that have been raised, it must be affirmed clearly that God transcends human sexuality. God *per se,* properly speaking, is neither male nor female since, as John reminds us, 'God is Spirit' (Jn 4:24). At the same time it must be acknowledged that the mystery of God is most appropriately represented from a human point of view in and through male and female images. In fact, God and divine action in the Judaeo-Christian tradition is presented in both male and female images (e.g. Dt 32:18; Is 42:14; Is 49:15; Is 66:13; Mt 13:33; Mt 23:37; Lk 15:8-10).

Given these observations there are no grounds for the exclusive use of male or female images of God. Indeed, the confinement of language about God to the exclusive use of male or female images runs the risk of distorting the full mystery of God. Ian Ramsey was fond of reminding his students that 'there is safety in numbers when it comes to models of God'. A variety and diversity of models can have the effect of enriching our understanding of the mystery and protecting us against the temptation to idolatry.

What this means in effect is that the revelation of God as Father must not be taken literally. The image of God as Father is symbolic and analogical. Like all symbols and analogies, it needs to be modified and enriched by other equally valid symbols and analogies such as God as Mother and God as Sister. In saying this, however, care must be taken to avoid simply adding female images to an already predominantly male understanding of God as can happen unthinkingly in remarks such as 'yes, God himself is (like) a mother'! Instead, the use of female images must be allowed to transform all our male images and *vice versa.* Equally, care must be taken not to simply complement masculine qualities with so-called feminine qualities. When this happens then our language can have the undesirable effect of endorsing particular stereotypes. What is required in both instances is a humble recognition and acceptance of the limits of all theological language. Only in this way do we truly arrive at a condition of 'learned ignorance' which respects the incomprehensible mystery of God.

Further, we need to point out in the context of the particular questions that have been raised, that the revelation of God as Father by Jesus is, as we have just seen, a repudiation of a patriarchal bias when it comes to a discussion about the mystery of God. The God whom Jesus reveals is a God who critiques and transforms all relationships of domination and subordination that characterise patriarchy. We have already noted that the Reign of God is about the re-establishment of right relationships in our world, the setting up of a new alternative community of radical equality and justice, between rich and poor, insider and outsider, young and old, women and men. This critique of patriarchy by Jesus is brought out in some of the parables. One particularly good example of this repudiation of patriarchy is the parable of the prodigal son (Lk 15:11-32). Many interpretations of this powerful parable have been put forward over the centuries. Most would agree today that it is as much a parable about the prodigal father as it is about the prodigal son. What is outstanding in this parable is the compassionate forgiveness and love of the father who goes out of his way to turn upside down the patriarchal relationship of superiority, dominance and power over the son. The son's expectation and projection upon his return home are typically patriarchal: submission, inferiority and servility. The father of the household, who in this parable images the forgiving love of God, transforms these patriarchal patterns, sets up a radically new relationship between the head of the household and the son, and calls for a celebration of this new situation.[13] The love and forgiveness of God, portrayed in this parable, clearly goes beyond a patriarchal interpretation of the revelation of God as Father.

If this non-patriarchal revelation of God as Father is to be fully reclaimed, then it becomes necessary that the image of God as

13 A more elaborate account of this patriarchal critique contained in the parable of the prodigal son can be found in S. Schneider, *Women and the Word*, pp. 46-48.

Father must be continually subjected to correction by other equally valid, non-patriarchal images of God like God as mother, lover and friend.[14] In particular, the image of God as Father must be transformed by the image of God as mother. The exclusion of female images from our understanding of God as Father in the past has often resulted in the reduction of this rich symbol to the endorsement of patriarchy. One of the great contributions of feminist theology in recent times has been a correction of this distortion.[15]

In the light of this emerging recovery of the non-patriarchal significance of the symbol of God as Father there is no reason why, as some have suggested, this symbol should be removed from the centre of christian faith. Surely the prominence of this symbol in scripture and tradition as well as in christology and trinitarian theology prevents any easy withdrawal of it from christianity. At the same time it is precisely the non-patriarchal character of the symbol of God as Father that obliges us to check and correct any simplistic tendency towards the absolutisation of the symbol.

One way of doing this is to attend, as recent research recommends, to the neglected but important 'I am' presentation of the God of Jesus in John's Gospel.[16] This perception of God by Jesus reverberates back to the revelation of God to Moses in terms of the ineffable 'I am who am/I will become what I become.' The mystery of God revealed to Moses and personified in the life of Jesus ultimately remains incomprehensible. It is this radical incomprehensibility of the mystery of God that requires us to respond to the questions posed about God as Father in the above way. The symbol of God as Father must not be taken literally, must not be interpreted as justifying patriarchy, and must not be

14 One example of how this can be done is developed in S. McFague, *Models of God*, London: SCM Press, 1987, chs. 4, 5 and 6.
15 See for example: E. Schussler Fiorenza, *In Memory of Her*, London: SCM Press, 1983; R.R. Reuther, *Sexism and God Talk: Towards a Feminist Theology*, London: SCM Press, 1983; A.E. Carr, *Transforming Grace: The Christian Tradition and Women's Experience*, New York: Harper & Row, 1988.
16 A helpful summary statement of this research can be found in Mary Collins "Naming God in Public Prayer", *Worship* 59 (1985) 291-304.

understood to commit christianity to the exclusive use of male images in theology.

Praxis and the Reign of God

The logic of our claim that the vision of the Reign of God is inspired to a large extent by Jesus' experience of God as Father implies that the coming of the Reign of God is similarly related to the praxis of Jesus. As we have already seen in chapter 1 Jesus closely associated the coming Reign of God, both in the present and in the future, with certain forms of human activity. These activities included bringing good news to the poor, sight to the blind, freedom to the oppressed, release to captives, and forgiveness to sinners. Activities like these are taken by Jesus as manifestations of the Reign of God 'come upon you' in the present as well as harbingers of its future realisation.

There are at least two significant points to be noted here concerning praxis and the Reign of God. First of all the existence of the Reign of God in the present is connected by Jesus with certain forms of human activity: justice, repentance, reconciliation, healing, and the alleviation of poverty. The second point is that these activities in the present have a bearing on the future realisation of the Kingdom.

Unfortunately, links between praxis and the Reign of God as well as the relationship between the present and the future, so prominent in the life of Jesus, have been largely severed down through the centuries. The reasons for this, both historical and theological, are extremely complex and difficult to unravel. These reasons would include at least reference to the gradual decline of the social and corporate dimensions of the Reign of God, the emergence of dualistic theologies of grace and history, and the development of *fuga mundi* (flight from the world) spiritualities.

In contrast, questions about the relationship between praxis and the Reign of God, between history and salvation, have returned to the centre of the theological stage today. Such questions are to the fore in the political and liberation theologies, in contemporary theologies of grace, and in eschatology. There is a growing unease among christians and theologians alike with responses that play down the presence of the Reign of God in the here and now, that diminish the role and responsibility of the christian community in promoting/advancing/contributing to the Reign of God, and that insist all the time on referring to the sinfulness of human nature and therefore its inability to respond to the challenge of the Reign of God.[17] Hasty charges of historical immanentism, Pelagianism and reductionism do not help to advance the christian conversation from either side in this debate.

Instead of prematurely assuming fixed doctrinal positions, we need to return to the preaching and praxis of Jesus concerning the Reign of God. This is not to suggest that the life of Jesus provides us with ready-made answers for twentieth-century questions but it does imply that the proclamation of Jesus concerning the Reign of God does give us an important point of departure for approaching the relationship between praxis and the Reign of God.

Within the proclamation of Jesus we find an explicit emphasis on the existence of the Reign of God in the present when certain things happen such as the promotion of justice, forgiveness, healing and reconciliation. The miracles of Jesus are portrayed in the New Testament as signs of the Reign of God in the present. Further, the preaching of Jesus points up the intrinsic connection that exists between these human activities and the future realisation of the Kingdom of God. The parables of Jesus talk about the image of sowing and harvesting (Mk 4:13-20), about the reading of the signs of the times in contrast to looking for signs from heaven, and the urgent need to act creatively now *(kairos)* rather than remain locked into present structures. What does emerge in the teaching of Jesus is that the Reign of God is redemptively co-active and co-present among those who hear and heed the call of Jesus to faith, repentance and a new liberating praxis.

It is in the light of these perspectives in the preaching of Jesus that contemporary theology talks about a proleptic, anticipatory, and analogical relationship existing between manifestations of the Reign

---

17 See G. Lohfink, 'The Exegetical Predicament concerning Jesus' Kingdom of God Proclamation', *Theology Digest*, 36 (1989), 103-110.

of God in this world and the realisation of the Reign of God in the future. Thus we find the Second Vatican Council suggesting that those who dedicate themselves to the earthly service of others 'make ready the material of the celestial realm by this ministry of theirs'.[18] Likewise Vatican II points out that 'the expectation of a new earth must not weaken but rather stimulate our concern for cultivating this one'[19] because those activities which are dedicated to the development and transformation of the world are 'able to give some kind of foreshadowing of the new age'.[20]

In other words there is an intrinsic link between those historical forms of praxis that promote the Reign of God in the present and its consummation in the future. To say this is not to deny that ultimately God is the one who, in the fullness of time, will effect the final realisation of the Reign of God in a manner that surpasses all human efforts. Instead, what is needed today is a recovery of the creative co-presence and co-activity of the Reign of God with humanity in present history as proclaimed by Jesus.

Further, it must be noted here that there is more than a hint in the preaching of Jesus that a real understanding of the Reign of God is available only in and through different forms of liberating praxis exercised by Jesus: feeding the hungry, healing the sick, removing injustice, and fostering table fellowship. It is within the paschal experience of participating in these and other forms of liberating praxis that a real grasp of the Reign of God is offered. The performance of action for justice is a praxis that opens the way to the Reign of God as gift and promise. We come to know God in and through the praxis of the Reign of God embodied in the life of Jesus: transforming injustice and suffering, bringing good news to the poor, and reconciling outsiders and insiders into a new community.

In other words, true knowledge of the Reign of God is not available through a spectator-type of epistemology, nor is it available simply through acquaintance with particular theories about God. Instead, a praxis epistemology concerning the Reign of God

18 G.S., a.38.
19 G.S., a.39.
20 G.S., a.39.

seems to be operative in the life of Jesus (e.g. Mt 7:21) and the early Church (e.g. 1 Co 4:20).[21] The presence of the Reign of God is disclosed principally through the praxis of liberation in the lives of women and men.

What is beginning to emerge from this brief reflection on praxis and the Reign of God is a particular understanding of God. The proclamation of the Reign of God is Jesus' way of talking about the nature of God. As we have already seen the God of the Reign of God is a radically relational God. We are now further discovering that the God of the Reign of God announced by Jesus is a God who is committed to altering the oppressive situation of people in society, a God who challenges the maintenance of the status quo when that status quo diminishes and demeans people. The God proclaimed by Jesus is primarily a healing and *salvator* God, and not therefore a guarantor or *conservator* God of the established and oppressive social order.[22]

The mission of Jesus is deliberately aimed at displacing a view of God which had been creeping in from Hellenistic religions, namely a view which allowed oppression of the poor to continue as if it were somehow divinely sanctioned. Jesus opposes this kind of thinking through his proclamation of the Reign of God and in doing so associates himself with the prophetic tradition of Judaism which refused to tolerate any easy alliance of injustice with religious faith (e.g. Am 5:21-25). The God of the Kingdom is a God who is for the individual: healing the sick, freeing the oppressed, liberating the little ones. Throughout his announcement of the coming Reign of God and the praxis it demands, 'Jesus unmasked the concept of God which enslaves people; he fought for a view of God as a God who liberates mankind, a view which has to be expressed in action'.[23]

---

21 For further details on a praxis-epistemology and its relationship to theology see D. Lane, *Foundations for a Social Theology: Praxis, Process and Salvation*, Dublin: Gill and Macmillan, 1984, pp. 72-74, and 'Praxis' in *New Catholic Encyclopedia*, vol. XVII, Supplement 1978-1988, Washington DC: Catholic University of America, 1989, pp. 390-394.

22 E. Schillebeeckx, *Interim Report on the Books 'Jesus' and 'Christ'*, London: SCM Press, 1980, p. 116.

23 Ibid., p. 131. See also pp. 8 and 99.

A Biblical Image of the Reign of God

By way of conclusion we need to gather these different aspects of the coming Reign of God into some kind of single perspective. Because the Reign of God is a multi-layered symbol as distinct from a symbol limited to a single meaning, it is almost impossible to capture the different levels of meaning in this rich symbol. In spite of this limitation we can say that the overriding biblical perspective on the Reign of God is that it is an eschatological symbol: it points towards the future, it promises new life to the earth and humanity, it is the object of Judaeo-Christian hope. As an eschatological symbol, it is consistently presented in Judaism, in the preaching and praxis of Jesus, and in the life of the Church through the image of a banquet. In Judaism, the end of time, the eschatological day of the Lord, is symbolised in terms of a banquet for all the nations:

> On this mountain the Lord will make for all peoples a feast of things, a feast of wine on the lees well refined. And he will destroy on this mountain the covering that is cast over all peoples, the veil that is spread over all nations, he will swallow up death for ever, and the Lord God will wipe away tears from all faces, and the reproaches of people he will take away from all the earth; for the Lord has spoken (Is 25:6-8).

This image of a banquet mediating the Reign of God is taken up explicitly in the preaching of Jesus when he points out that 'many will come from east and west to sit at the table with Abraham, Isaac and Jacob in the Kingdom' (Mt 8:11; see also Lk 13:29). More specifically, Jesus likens the coming Reign of God to a man who 'once gave a great banquet and invited many' (Lk 14:16). In particular, the many meals that Jesus had with his disciples, with tax collectors, sinners and others, are understood as messianic signs of the coming Reign of God. For example, the feeding of the five thousand in the desert (Jn 6:1-15) is interpreted by the crowd in eschatological terms:

> When people saw the sign which he had done, they said, 'this is indeed the prophet who is to come into the world' (Jn 6:14).

John goes on to note that the crowd 'were about to come and take him by force to make him king' (Jn 6:15). Clearly, a symbolic and messianic connection is established in the ministry of Jesus between his many meals of table-fellowship and the banquet that symbolises the coming Reign of God. It is within the context of these meals in the ministry of Jesus and their eschatological promise that we can turn to the Last Supper. The Last Supper was the last in a series of messianic meals which had taken place in the life of Jesus. Further, the Last Supper occurred significantly in or around the time of the Jewish Passover. It is this double context that provides us with the proper ambiance for understanding the institution of the Eucharist and its direct relationship to the Reign of God.

On the one hand the Eucharist is more than just another meal added to the meals and ministry of Jesus. The institution of the Eucharist introduces the new elements of sacrifice and covenant: 'my blood of the covenant, which is poured out for many' (Mk 14:24). On the other hand we find Jesus in Mark and Matthew going on immediately *after* the words of institution to say:

> Truly, I say to you, I shall not drink again of the fruit of the vine until that day when I drink it new in the Kingdom of God (Mk 14:25; see Mt 26:29).

This verse suggests a direct link between the Eucharist and the Reign of God. Without going into the meaning of the Eucharist as sacrifice, memorial and covenant which is beyond the purpose of this chapter, it should be clear for our limited purposes here that the Eucharist is the sacrament of the messianic banquet of the Reign of God: it gathers the disciples of Christ into a new communion, it recalls the death and resurrection of Jesus as the founding event of the Reign of God in the world, it nourishes the pilgrim people *en route* to the Kingdom, it anticipates the future unity and glory of humanity in the Reign of God, and it unites disciples into a posture of praise and thanksgiving offered to God our Father through the mediation of Jesus Christ in the power of the Spirit as an essential element in their belonging to the Reign of God. It is John's Gospel in particular that makes explicit this link between the Eucharist and the Reign of God:

> He who eats my flesh and drinks my blood has eternal life, and I will raise him up on the last day (Jn 6:54).

For John and the early Church the Eucharist is the pledge and promise of eternal life in the Reign of God. It is the celebration of the Eucharist above all else that mediates and realises the transforming power and co-presence of the Reign of God in our world today in preparation for God's tomorrow. To be sure, there are other signs of the Reign of God in our midst, but it is the Eucharist as instituted by Christ that effects sacramentally the Reign of God in the world because it is the Eucharist that brings the forgiveness, peace and unity which are the enduring qualities of the future Reign of God.

3

The Cross of Christ as the Revelation of God

A characteristic of contemporary christology has been the recovery of the importance and centrality of the resurrection of Jesus. This welcome emphasis on the resurrection is one of the many fruits of the renewal in biblical studies since Vatican II. Advances in theology, as in most other areas of life, have a price. Some christologies now have become so preoccupied with the resurrection that they have neglected other important aspects of the mystery of Christ. One such aspect is the cross of Christ. Quite often, insufficient attention is given to the death of Jesus in contemporary christologies. In some instances the resurrection of Jesus is allowed to swallow up the cross. In others the death of Jesus appears merely as 'a passing phase' or 'a transit station' in the history of salvation and yet in all the gospels the passion narratives are to the fore.

Of course, there are other reasons too for the relative neglect of the cross of Christ in contemporary theology. For one thing the message of the resurrection is more attractive and consoling than the cross. The cross, when taken seriously, is a scandal and so we frequently tend to cover over the crown of thorns with a cluster of roses (Goethe). Another reason for the demise of the cross is that much of the language describing the significance of the death of Jesus is culturally alien to modern experience. Symbols like 'ransom', 'expiation', 'blood-sacrifice', 'satisfaction', and some of the theologies implicit in them, are unattractive to twentieth-century sensibilities.

Perhaps more serious is the fact that this neglect of the cross in christology can and does give rise to distortions in our understanding of the resurrection of Jesus. For example, the resurrection without the cross tends to generate a kind of naive optimism about the future in contrast to the cruciform character of christian hope. Further, a theology of resurrection unrestrained by the cross can end up presenting the resurrection as an appendix to the end of life rather than a challenge intrinsic to the way we live present existence. In addition, a resurrection-centred christology which bypasses the cross has very little to say to the pain and agony, the tragedy and failure, the suffering and dying which are a common feature of universal human experience.

In the light of these rather general observations it is not too surprising to find the 1985 Extraordinary Synod of Bishops in Rome calling for a development of a 'theology of the cross'.[1] The context of this call is the present signs of the times which the Synod points out 'are somewhat different from those existing at the time of the Council'. Today, it is noted, 'there is a growing amount of hunger, oppression, injustice and war, torture and terrorism, and other forms of violence'.[2]

For these reasons it seems appropriate in this chapter to explore some of the historical and theological significance of the cross of Christ. For the Christian, the cross ought to be a distinctive mark of any theology of Christian discipleship.

The Cross in the Life of Jesus

The obvious starting point for any discussion of the cross must be a clear affirmation of the absolute unity that exists between the death and resurrection. The resurrection is not another event in addition to the death of Jesus. Instead, the resurrection is, as it were, the other side of the death of Jesus. In saying this, however, we must be careful not to collapse the resurrection of Jesus into the death of Jesus or vice versa. Within the unity that exists between the death and resurrection of Jesus there is a distinction: the death of Jesus is

1 *Synod Report: The Final Report and Message to the People of God*, London: CTS 1986, Section D.2.
2 Ibid. Section D.1.

a special moment in itself which leads to and results in the resurrection of Christ. Likewise, the resurrection is not simply a response to or an interpretation of the death of Jesus. Rather, it is a distinct 'happening' consequent upon the death of Jesus. The breakdown of the cross is the context of the breakthrough in the resurrection.

Having asserted this unity-within-distinction of the death and resurrection of Jesus we must also affirm the close relationship that exists between the historical life of Jesus, his death on the cross, and the resurrection. It is only within the context of what went before the death of Jesus and what came after in terms of the resurrection and the gift of the Spirit that we can begin to probe the mystery of the cross. If the cross of Christ has been neglected, it is often because this fundamental unity within the life of Jesus has been fragmented.

Consistent with these principles an outline sketch must be given of the historical life of Jesus by way of introduction to the cross. Most commentators agree that one of the primary categories for understanding the historical life of Jesus is that of seeing Jesus as the Spirit-filled, eschatological prophet. Jesus appears as the prophet of the end of time led by the Spirit of God (Lk 4:16-30), calling people to faith, repentance and conversion.

The over-arching horizon of this prophetic ministry is the announcement of the Reign of God as present gift and future promise. The coming into being of the Reign of God is presented by Jesus in terms of founding a new and alternative community of right relationships. The shape of this community is outlined in the beatitudes. A reversal of values is envisaged whereby the greatest are those who serve, the poor are given priority, and those who lose their lives as disciples for the Reign of God will save them. At the centre of this alternative community we find the dynamic presence of a caring, compassionate and forgiving God bringing about a new justice, peace and love in the world.

What is outstanding about the life of Jesus is his particular experience and understanding of God. Jesus' intense and permanent experience of God as *Abba*/Father in prayer and praxis marks him out as quite unique within the history of Israel. It is on the basis of this profound experience that Jesus understands himself as Son of God sent (Mt 10:40; Lk 10:16) to herald the imminent Reign of God. Further, it is this co-experience of God as Father that is the foundation of his understanding of the graciousness of God's co-presence in the world summed up in the announcement of the Reign of God.

It is against this background of Jesus' prophetic ministry, his proclamation of the Reign of God and his unique experience of God as Father that we can begin to approach the death of Jesus. As a prophet Jesus must have reckoned with the imminent possibility of his own death. Equally his radical preaching about the Reign of God would have brought him into some conflict with the religious and civil authorities of the day. Likewise the theological implications of his religious experience of God as *Abba*/Father would have alerted him to the potential misunderstanding that his vision would provoke. At the same time the prospect of death must have threatened the mission and ministry of Jesus with failure. Jesus, therefore, had to struggle with the apparent negativity of death alongside his Spirit-filled experience and understanding of his calling as prophet and as Son sent by God the Father.

The Death of Jesus on the Cross

Allowing for the human and historical circumstances that brought about his death – such as the journey up to Jerusalem, the incident in the temple, the seeming complicity between synagogue and state, the trial – it must be admitted with J. Moltmann and others that the real drama of the cross centres around the experience taking place between Jesus as Son and God as Father. The question of death which Jesus must face is ultimately a question about his relationship with God as Father. Up to now Jesus had come to know and experience God in a unique way. God as Father was experienced by Jesus as personally active and creatively present in his mission and ministry.

Fidelity to his experience of God as Father and the radical implications of this experience in terms of the coming Reign of God seem to bring Jesus closer to death and indeed appear to call into question his mission. The major issue facing Jesus is how to reconcile the richness of his religious experience up to now with the pending emptiness of death and how to bring together his mission for the Reign of God with the apparent futility of a premature ending. The gospel narrative of the passion and death of Jesus is a witness to the resolution of these painful paradoxes within the life of Jesus. Two examples will suffice to illustrate this point.

On the one hand the negativity of death is transformed by Jesus into something positive associated with the coming Reign of God – a change that is not inconsistent with the other reversals associated with the Reign of God. The only positive way left for the coming of the Reign of God is the awesome way of death. Death is reluctantly accepted by Jesus as somehow bound up with the coming Reign of God. This new sense of direction in the life of Jesus is glimpsed at the last supper when he says to his disciples: 'I tell you I shall not drink again of this fruit of the vine until that day when I drink it new with you in my Father's kingdom' (Mt 26:29). Here, a positive connection is established between the coming Reign of God and the imminent death of Jesus. This positive connection would have been made possible in part through Jesus' awareness of the suffering servant theme in Isaiah.

On the other hand the apparent abandonment of Jesus by God the Father in suffering and death on the cross is overcome by the prayerful recitation of Psalm 22 by Jesus on the cross. The words 'My God, My God, why have you forsaken me' (Mt 27:46) are merely the opening lines of this psalm. The rest of the psalm, which we can presume was well-known to Jesus, moves from absence to presence, from loss to gain, from complaint to praise in regard to the mystery of God. To be sure, according to all outward appearances God seems to have forsaken Jesus. At the same time, however, the prayerful recitation of Psalm 22 for help uttered by Jesus goes beyond his apparent aloneness in death.

That Jesus does experience a deep sense of abandonment and forsakenness by God on the cross is clearly communicated by the gospel accounts. The God whom Jesus had dared to call

Abba/Father has suddenly become silent. The God whose presence Jesus had heralded as near and imminent now seems sadly absent. The God in whose name Jesus had performed mighty deeds now appears to be strangely impotent. The preaching and praxis of Jesus, externally speaking, is called into question. The mission and ministry of Jesus seem to have reached a painful point of collapse on the cross. The coming Reign of God is abruptly ended. The divine silence surrounding the cross signals outwardly a sense of failure and tragedy. This apparent abandonment by God the Father is in turn compounded by the abandonment of Jesus by most of his disciples. Different forces of evil – personal, social, political and religious – seem to coalesce into a kind of cosmic destruction of the man Jesus. And yet, in the midst of this dark and desolate experience Jesus trustingly surrenders himself in faith, hope and love to God the Father who had initiated, sustained and enriched his mission and ministry.

No amount of talk subsequently about the resurrection can remove this extraordinary historical experience of Jesus in Gethsemane and at Golgotha. To be sure, the suffering and death of Jesus can be passed over, played down, forgotten, even ignored by a subsequent highlighting of the resurrection. But, when this happens, as already noted, the resurrection of Jesus becomes distorted in one way or another. Indeed, the identity of the risen Christ is destroyed once we forget the cross because the risen Christ *is* always the crucified Christ. Further, when we choose to forget about the cross we end up ignoring a central aspect of the revelation of God in Jesus. What happens all too frequently in christology is that we interpret the death of Jesus in theories of expiation, satisfaction and ransom that fail to incorporate the new revelation of God that took place on the cross. Only when we grasp the strange character of God's revelation on the cross can we begin to interpret the saving significance of the death of Jesus in categories transformed by that unique event.

What this means, in effect, is that we must reflect on the starkness of the cross without allowing the glory of the resurrection to distract us from the climax of salvation history in the event of the cross. This does not mean that we ignore the significance of the resurrection or its revelatory impact. Instead, it implies that by reflecting on the cross we will be preparing the way for a proper appreciation of the resurrection. Only by attending to the cross in the light of the resurrection and to the resurrection in the shadow of the cross can we begin to grasp the unified meaning of the saving death and resurrection of Jesus. The best example of this approach is to be found in the writings of Paul who not only highlights the unity of the death and resurrection but also manages to work out distinct theologies of the cross and of the resurrection. A short overview of Paul's theology seems appropriate at this stage.

Paul's Theology of the Cross

To appreciate Paul's thinking about the cross we should keep in mind his prior persecution of the early christians and the theological factors motivating this persecution. Paul's stance against the christians is provoked by a number of complex factors: the messianic claims being made about Jesus by the early Church, the suggestion that the so-called Messiah had been condemned to death on the cross by the law, the admission of gentiles without circumcision into the chosen people of God. These factors can be summed up in the Jewish charge: 'Cursed be everyone who dies on a tree' (Ga 3:13). The real issue for Paul the Jew against the early Church is a clash between the law and a crucified Messiah. If the law is responsible for the death of Jesus, then he cannot be the true Messiah.

The conversion of Paul turns upside down the theological thinking of Paul the Jew. Paul the christian now accepts the unity of the death and resurrection of Jesus put forward in the creedal statements of the early Church (1 Co 15:3-5; Rm 4:24-25; 8:34; 2 Co 5:15; 1 Th 4:14). It is on the basis of these foundational statements of christian identity that Paul goes on to develop his own distinctive and complementary theologies of the cross and of the resurrection.

The ingredients of his theology of the cross are threefold. On the one hand he states clearly that from now on: 'I decided to know nothing among you except Jesus Christ and him crucified' (1 Co

2:2). In the light of the resurrection, the death of Jesus is now seen as a judgment on the world: 'since...the world did not know God through wisdom, it pleased God through the folly of what we preach to save those who believe' (1 Co 1:21). In particular, the death of Jesus is a victory over the powers of darkness operative in this world. For Paul the death of Christ frees us from sin (2 Co 5:21), from the flesh (Rm 8:3-8), from death (Rm 6:1-10), and from the law (Ga 3:10-13; 4:4-5).

In virtue of this Paul goes on to say that the crucified Christ 'is a stumbling block to the Jews and folly to the gentiles' because 'Jews demand signs and the Greeks seek wisdom' (1 Co 1:23, 22). Within Judaism the law was everything, and for Greek culture rationality was the guiding norm. The cross of Christ contradicts these two pillars of ancient civilisation, becoming a scandal to the religious Jews and a defiance to the philosophical Greeks of this world.

This in turn enables Paul to declare that the cross of Christ reveals 'the power of God and the wisdom of God. For the foolishness of God is wiser than men, and the weakness of God is stronger than men' (1 Co 1:24-25). Paul presents the cross as the great reversal of everything revered in the old world. To the worldly-wise, the cross is a clear contradiction of all they have learned, and to the religiously minded Jews, it is a scandal to their sense of election and righteousness. It is almost as if Paul goes out of his way to confuse and to shock people with the cross. Out of this apparent confusion comes a new kind of perception which is able to see strength in weakness and not just after weakness (2 Co 12:10), light in darkness and not just after darkness, and life in death and not just after death. (Rm 6:3-4; 2 Co 4:11; 2 Co 6:9).

In effect, Paul's distinctive theology of the cross is remarkable for the paradoxes and contrasting opposites that it is able to hold together in a creative tension. Equally significant is the suggestive way he is able to associate the cross of Christ with the revelation of God taking place on Calvary. The cross reveals the unique power, wisdom and love of God (1 Co 1:24). Yet, this particular emphasis of Paul is one of the least developed within classical christology. The revelation of God on the cross ought to have changed dramatically the Judaeo-Hellenistic understanding of the mystery of God. To be sure it did so in terms of the trinitarian understanding of God. However, it must be acknowledged that the trinitarian understanding of God developed more by way of reflection on the divinity of Jesus and the doctrine of the Incarnation, and less as a result of reflection on the historical revelation of God that took place on the cross of Jesus. Furthermore, certain forms of the trinitarian doctrine have tended to leave the christian God detached from the dynamics of history in spite of the christian doctrine of the Incarnation. Many would hold that the reason for this detachment of the Christian doctrine of God from salvation-history was an excessive reliance on the cold and seemingly static categories of Greek philosophy: immutability, impassibility, omnipotence. Thus, we find Karl Barth arguing that it is not enough to add christology to the Aristotelian notion of God. Instead, the revelation of God in Christ must be allowed to 'break up and reform' the Aristotelian understanding of God.[3] Likewise Walter Kasper points out: 'The christian...understanding of God in the light of Jesus' cross and resurrection leads to a crisis, even a revolution, in the way of seeing God'.[4] Similarly, John F. Haught notes: 'The image of the "crucified God" is central to Christian teaching, though perhaps it has not been taken seriously. Instead, "God" has been ensconced, in classical theologies, as omnipotently immune to suffering and tragedy'.[5] This new way of understanding God in the light of Christ, (e.g. the *Abba* experience, the vision of the Reign of God in the parables and praxis of Jesus, the cross and resurrection) is one of the major challenges facing christian theology today. The Hellenistic understanding of God continues to dominate christian thought and action about God without taking adequate account of the revelatory impact of the Christ-event. In particular, the significance of the cross for a specifically christian understanding of God needs to be brought much more to the fore. This is all the more true in virtue of the break with Jewish theology and Hellenistic philosophy which

3   *Church Dogmatics*, Edinburgh: T. & T. Clark, 1969-1980, II/1, p. 495.
4   *Jesus the Christ*, London: Burns and Oates, 1976, p. 168.
5   J.F. Haught, *The Cosmic Adventure: Science, Religion and the Quest for Purpose*, New York: Paulist Press, 1984, p. 165.

Paul attributes to the cross of Christ (1 Co 1:22-24). Contemporary theologians (e.g. E. Jüngel, W. Kasper, J. Moltmann) emphasise the cross of Christ as the final self-revelation of God.

The Cross and the Revelation of God

Obviously, we cannot work out here all the details of a christian rethinking of God in the light of the cross. Yet, some 'half hints and guesses' might be hazarded here. First of all it must be pointed out in virtue of the cross that God is revealed to be most active and present in those situations where God, at least externally, appears to be inactive and absent. The particular presence and activity of God in Judaism is universalised by the cross of Christ. The presence of God in the law and the temple is relativised by the symbol of the cross. There is no area of life now that falls outside the presence and activity of God. In the cross, God is found to be active and present in the midst of extraordinary evil, suffering and death – drawing good out of evil, salvation out of suffering, and new life out of death. The realms of human failure and tragedy are now revealed to be within the compass of divine activity and transformation. In its own way the cross of Christ captures the paradox in life that those moments in which God seems most absent can be recognised as moments in which God is most present. The silence of God at Calvary does not denote absence. Instead, silence and signs, darkness and light, suffering and joy are now equally the location of God's creative presence and activity.

Secondly, this dark presence and activity of God in the death of Christ puts an end once and for all to the suggestion that God is indifferent to the pain and suffering of humanity. The Greek quality of apathy *(apatheia)* given by philosophers to God can no longer be attributed to the christian God. The God revealed in the cross of Jesus is a God who is moved and touched by the suffering and death inflicted by humanity on Jesus. God the Father is not indifferent to the suffering and death of his Son. In the cross God the Father became vulnerable to the suffering and death of his Son Jesus, and through Jesus God the Father remains vulnerable to the suffering and death of humanity.

At a time when we hear so much about apathy in the world towards religion in general and christianity in particular, we need to question the reasons for this apathy. Is it possible that the classical image of God as 'apathetic' has something to do with this peculiarly contemporary phenomenon of apathy? Is there some causal connection between an apathetic theology and an apathetic people? Apathy as an attribute of God cannot be grounded in the historical revelation of God in Judaism and in Jesus.

In the light of these observations we need to analyse more fully what it means to say that the cross of Christ is the Revelation of God to the world. As we have already seen, Paul puts us on notice that we are dealing here with a Revelation which is perceived as a scandal to the Jews and folly to the Greeks. It is quite clear that we are describing a Revelation that is paradoxical in character: presence in silence, power in weakness, and light in darkness.

The Revelation of God on the cross stands out as a radical critique of both theism and atheism. In the first instance it is a critique of those forms of theism such as deism which remove God from personal involvement in the world, especially in the area of suffering. In the second instance, the cross is also a critique of those forms of atheism which cannot believe in a loving God who is indifferent to the suffering of the world. To say that the cross of Christ is the Revelation of God is to imply that God in some way or other is affected by human suffering.

If we accept with St Paul that God was in Christ reconciling the world unto himself, then we cannot draw back from saying that the same God was in Christ suffering on the cross. The removal of God from personal association with the suffering and death of Christ could have the effect of denying the cross of its saving significance; it could also end up reducing the cross to the level of just another human tragedy. Instead we wish to claim here that in the cross of Christ God experiences suffering.

To suggest that God suffers in Christ – that God experiences suffering on the cross – is to suggest something that transforms the classical understanding of the mystery of God. The cross of Christ clearly calls into question the existence of a God who is simply or primarily or exclusively immutable and impassible. It is not enough to reply here that Christ suffered only in his human nature without the personal involvement of his divine nature, nor is it sufficient to suggest that the transcendence of God remains untouched by the historical events of Calvary. It is difficult to see how these responses, and others like them, do justice to the unity of God in Christ defined by the Councils of Nicea (325) and Ephesus (431), the oneness of the person of Christ declared by the Council of Chalcedon (451), and the underlying meaning of the Incarnation.

Thus we find Rahner pointing out that:

> If it is said that the incarnate logos died only in his human reality, and if this is tacitly understood to mean that this death did not affect God, then only half the truth has been stated. The really christian truth has been omitted.[6]

In an equally explicit manner we find Lonergan saying:

> It would seem contrary to the faith to hold that it was not the only Son of God the Father that suffered but a human soul, a human body, a human consciousness, or a human subject not identical with the Son of God.[7]

It is precisely at this point that we come up against the peculiar character of the Revelation of God that was taking place in the passion and death of Jesus. The Revelation in question is not one of displaying divine power through power (omnipotence) but one of divine power breaking through in weakness, nor is it one of the divine unmoved mover remaining unmoved (immutability) but one of divine being becoming historically involved, nor is it one of invulnerability (impassibility) remaining aloof through detachment but one of divine perfection revealing itself through self-emptying on the cross *(kenosis)*. In the life, passion and death of Jesus, the love of God enters fully into the human condition (at-one-ment) and this divine self-emptying, better, this Incarnation of the love of God,

6 K. Rahner, "Jesus Christ", *Encyclopedia of Theology: A Concise Sacramentum*, K. Rahner (ed.), London: Burns & Oates, 1975, p. 770.
7 B. Lonergan, *Collection*, London: Darton, Longman and Todd, 1967, p. 193 n.51.

involves a real, personal and historical experience of suffering in God. The cross is at the heart of the Christian mystery and it must be admitted that this extraordinary truth does indeed challenge all our philosophical images and symbols of God. Indeed, it seems to threaten the very dignity and transcendence of the mystery of God. As soon as we say that God experiences suffering, a host of other questions arise. Can a God who suffers, still be God? Does a suffering God diminish the meaning and mystery of God? Is the essence of God something that must be removed from suffering? What is the significance of the suffering of God in Christ for our understanding of suffering today? There are at least two issues at stake here and these concern the perfection of God and the very nature of God. *end of reading*

The first issue concerns our understanding of the perfection of God. Is the perfection of God compromised by the suggestion of suffering within God? For the Greeks it was the perfection of God, which excluded all change and therefore suffering, that distinguished and separated God from a humanity who is subject all the time to change and therefore by implication to suffering. The objective of the Greek position here, namely safeguarding the Mystery of God in its perfection, is surely both desirable and necessary in any discussion about the Mystery of God. Can this objective, however, be realised more credibly in and through a conceptuality different from that of Greek philosophy, a conceptuality that is more in touch with the contemporary experience and understanding of men and women in the world? Might it not be suggested that the perfection of God revealed in the Bible is something that implies personal contact by God with the suffering of humanity?

There can be no doubt that our experience and understanding of the world will shape and influence our experience and understanding of the Mystery of God. In contrast to the Greek perception of the world, a contemporary understanding, informed by such diverse areas as the new physics, ecology, feminism, and process philosophy, suggests a universe that is at once dynamic, organic and relational. This emerging framework implies the co-existence of a God who is personally related to the world without necessarily being diminished by this relatedness. Indeed, the reality of God as Love, as we shall see in a moment, would seem to demand this kind of inter-relatedness, and therefore by implication some involvement with suffering. Within this dynamic and organic framework there would seem to be room for the co-presence of a God who affects the world and is affected by the world in a manner that does not compromise the perfection of God. Such a God, in contrast to the seemingly detached and apathetic God of Greek philosophy, would be a God of empathy and solidarity with the world. The idea of the existence of a God of pathos is one that is not altogether alien to the God of the Jewish and christian scriptures, as we shall also see below.

The second issue here concerns the very nature of God as a saving God. Can we posit a God who saves, which we must do when talking about the God of the Judaeo-christian tradition, who at the same time is not touched by human suffering? Surely a God who takes the suffering of humanity into God's own heart is more credible than a God who exists outside the stream of human suffering? Can we not appeal here to the soteriological principle of the early Fathers of the Church who pointed out that 'what is not assumed is not redeemed'? Does this principle not imply that God as saviour in Christ took on the suffering of the world? Is not this part of the meaning of D. Bonhoeffer's compelling claim that 'only a suffering God can help us'?

Further, whatever can be said about the permanently disturbing and troubling question of suffering is surely more credible if it can be said in a way that includes reference to God's personal experience and understanding of suffering from the inside. Is not the real point of the cross to be found in the belief that God takes on the mystery of human suffering from 'the inside out', as it were?

On the basis of these observations it seems possible in the light of the cross, indeed necessary, to talk about a God who experiences suffering without however diminishing the Mystery of God. Given the perspectives implicit in these observations on the perfection and nature of God, it seems difficult to see how God in the light of the cross can continue to be understood as a God who is indifferent to or uninvolved in the suffering of humanity.[8]

Given the suggestion that God is involved with human suffering in Christ the question arises: Is the suffering of God in Christ on the cross an exception or does it tell us something about the nature of God's permanent presence in the world? The answer to this question depends on how we see the relationship between the Mystery of Christ and the Mystery of God. In this regard we suggest that christology is a form of concentrated creation.[9] What happens in the Mystery of Christ is at least a crystalisation of what is happening in the world around us. Christology is a microcosm of what is taking place in the macrocosm of creation itself. As Tertulian remarks:

> Whatever was the form and expression which was given to the clay (by the Creator), Christ, one day to become man, was in his thoughts.[10]

One of the principal fruits of christology in this century arising out of a return to the scriptures and a dialogue with other world religions, has been the emergence of an inclusive christology in contrast to the existence of an exclusivist christology of former times. Not only is christology a microcosm of creation but it must also be affirmed that the crucified and risen Christ is creation brought to fulfilment.

In the light of this close relation between Christ and creation we suggest that the cross of Christ reveals the suffering of God in creation and that this suffering of God in the world is not something that simply began at Golgotha.

The theologian who has dealt most explicitly with the question of suffering in God is Jürgen Moltmann and yet there appears to be a real tension in the writings of Moltmann on this particular point. On

8   For a helpful but different treatment of the impassibility of God see G.O. Hanlon, 'Does God Change? H.U. von Balthasar on the Immutability of God', *Irish Theological Quarterly* 53 (1987), 161-183.
9   See E. Schillebeeckx, *The Interim Report*, London: SCM Press, pp. 126-128. A similar understanding of christology, based on Paul, Irenaeus, Scotus, de Chardin and Rahner, can be found in D. Lane, *The Reality of Jesus*, Dublin: Veritas Publications, 1975, pp. 134-141.
10   *De resurrectione mortuorum*, 6. (*P.L.* 2, 282).

the one hand Moltmann, in his early writings, seems to suggest that something new took place on the cross and that this something new constituted the beginning of the history of suffering in the life of the Blessed Trinity. In *The Crucified God*, Moltmann states that 'God has made the suffering of the world his own in the cross of his Son'[11] and that 'the trinitarian God-event on the cross becomes the history of God'.[12] At the same time, however, Moltmann also talks about the suffering of God that can be found within the history of Judaism in virtue of God's covenant with his people and the suffering of God that goes back ultimately to the act of creation *ex nihilo*. For instance, in *The Crucified God* he claims that 'the pathos of God perceived and proclaimed by the prophets is the pre-supposition for the christian understanding of the living God from the passion of Christ'.[13] There is, therefore, something of a tension in Moltmann between the particular suffering of God on the cross and the universal suffering of God in the world. In his writings after *The Crucified God*, Moltmann moves towards a partial resolution of this tension. In *The Trinity and the Kingdom of God* he talks quite explicitly about the self-limitation and humiliation of God[14] that begins in creation: 'the divine *Kenosis* which begins with the creation of the world reaches its perfected and completed form in the Incarnation of the Son'.[15] In a later book, *God in Creation,* he goes on further to say: 'The cross is the Mystery of creation'.[16]

What is significant about Moltmann is that he moves backwards from the suffering of God in Christ on the cross to the suffering of God in Judaism and in creation. An equally valid approach to the suffering of God in the world, especially for someone perhaps less shy of natural theology than Moltmann is, would be to move from creation to the cross as the concentration of creation. If we acknowledge the full gift of human freedom given by God to

11 J. Moltmann, *The Crucified God*, London: SCM Press, 1974, p. 277.
12 Ibid. p. 255.
13 Ibid. p. 275. See also 'The Passion of God' in *The Trinity and the Kingdom of God*, London: SCM Press, 1981.
14 *The Trinity and the Kingdom of God*, London: SCM Press, 1981, pp. 39, 118.
15 Ibid. p. 118.
16 *God in Creation: An Ecological Doctrine of Creation*, London: SCM Press, 1985, p. 91.

human beings in the act of creation, then we must also recognise that this implies some form of freely chosen self-limitation by God in creation.[17] The divine act of creation is itself a divine act of self-emptying love *(kenosis)* in virtue of the gift of human freedom endowed upon humanity. Now this divine act of self-emptying love is wounded by sin from the beginning of time: 'And the Lord was sorry he had made man on the earth, and it grieved him to his heart' (Gn 6:6). In spite of the fall and failure of humanity, the initial act of self-emptying love in creation is continued and extended in the covenant between God and the people of Israel. Both activities of self-emptying love imply a real relationship between God and creation, and between God and Israel. This initial relationship of love between God and creation and Israel is the foundation of the personal relationship between God and Jesus in the Trinitarian event of the cross. John Macquarrie captures the point we are making in the following way:

> In creating an existent other than himself, and in granting to that existent a measure of freedom and autonomy, God surrendered any unclouded bliss that might have belonged to him had he remained simply wrapped up in his own perfection. In creating, he consents to know the pain and frustration of the world. All this needs to be strongly asserted against the teaching of divine impassibility presented in traditional theism.[18]

It is the prophets of the Hebrew scriptures who capture in colourful terms some of the drama resulting from this living relationship of Yahweh with creation and his people. We find many of the prophets, for example Amos, Jeremiah and Isaiah, describing the sorrow, disappointment and suffering of Yahweh with his people. Further, according to the Jewish scholar Abraham Heschel it is not so much that the prophets have received a particular revelation about God's suffering but rather that they are the ones who in virtue of their relationship with Yahweh can sense the

---

17 This point is carefully argued by L. Gilkey in *Reaping the Whirlwind*, New York: Seabury Press, 1976, pp. 249 and 279.
18 J. Macquarrie, *In Search of Deity: An Essay in Dialectical Theism*, London: SCM Press, 1984, p. 180. See the helpful commentary by Gabriel Daly on this quotation from Macquarrie in *Creation and Redemption*, Dublin: Gill and Macmillan, 1988, pp. 24-25.

suffering of Yahweh. For Heschel the prophet is one who speaks out of sympathy with the pathos of God.[19] Heschel gives the example of Isaiah 42:14 which likens the suffering of Yahweh to 'a woman in travail' and he also notes how according to Isaiah 63:9, 'in all their affliction, he (Yahweh) was afflicted'. One commentator goes so far as to suggest that the suffering of God expressed in Jeremiah 45 gives us 'a glimpse of the eternal cross in the heart of God'[20] – a remark that might be reserved more properly to the death of Christ on the cross.

Attention to this neglected aspect of the Hebrew scriptures will help us to come to grips with the divine drama taking place on the cross at Calvary. Within this perspective the suffering of God in Christ on the cross no longer appears simply as some exception or isolated incident in the historical life of God. Instead, the suffering of God in Christ on the cross gathers up a reality already present in the history of Yahweh's relationship with Israel. In other words, the pathos of God in creation and in history is personalised in Christ on the cross. In effect the suffering of God in Christ on the cross picks up the perennial question about the meaning of suffering in the world as expressed in the Book of Job.

What is now beginning to emerge is that the passion of God for humanity in the world and the passion of humanity for God in history coincide in the suffering and death of Christ on the cross. The search of God for humanity reaches its fullest, self-emptying expression of love on the cross.

In other words, the loving outreach of God initiated in creation *ex nihilo* and extended in the history of Israel comes to full term in the cross of Christ. At the same time, humanity's quest for unity with God, summed up in the life of Christ, ends in the painful experience of godforsakenness by Christ on the cross. The cry of godforsakenness by Christ on the cross strikingly echoes the bewildered protest of Job against suffering in the world.

Divine self-emptying and human forsakenness coalesce in the

19 A. Heschel. *The Prophets.* New York: Harper & Row, 1962, pp. 308-314.
20 H. Wheeler Robinson. *The Cross in the Old Testament.* London: SCM Press, 1955, p. 185.

drama of Calvary. The cross reveals the self-emptying love of God in the world *ab initio:* the God of Jesus Christ is a God who suffers out of love for humanity and the world. This revelation of God is also at the same time a revelation about the kind of world we live in: there is suffering at the heart of the universe we inhabit and this presence of cosmic suffering is exposed on the cross. What Virgil once called 'the tears of things' which lie at the centre of the world have been disclosed in the agony of the cross. The historic cross therefore lays bare something of the flawed character of the cosmic process as well as the sinful condition of humanity.

An additional point arising out of this analysis, that should be made at least in passing about the revelation of the suffering love of God in Christ on the cross, is the following. The cross not only lights up our understanding of the historical suffering of God in creation and in the history of Israel but it also lights up the ongoing suffering love of God in the body of Christ today and in the history of humanity until He comes in glory. The coming of God in glory has been prefigured eschatologically in the death and resurrection of Christ. Between the First and Second Coming of Christ, God ,out of love, continues to suffer in the world. The Second Coming of Christ involves not only the transformation of humanity and creation but also the final glorification of God in the overcoming of all suffering.

Further, in saying the cross reveals the ongoing suffering love of God in the world, care must be taken not to imply in any way that God is responsible for human suffering or, even worse, that the cross gives us a reason for accepting suffering passively or at least an explanation for suffering in the world. The cross of Christ is neither a justification nor an explanation of the awful suffering that continues to tear our world apart. At most the cross helps us to live in hope with suffering and to realise at the same time that we do not suffer alone or in vain. In particular the cross of Christ forces us to hear in a new way the striking story of Elie Wiesel, a Jewish survivor of the Holocaust, given in his book *Night:*

> The SS hung two Jewish men and a boy before the assembled inhabitants of the camp. The men died quickly but the death

> struggle of the boy lasted half an hour. 'Where is God? Where is he?', a man behind me asked...I heard the man cry again 'Where is God now?' and I heard a voice within me answer, 'Here he is – he is hanging here on the gallows.'[21]

The silence of God in the face of suffering is not a silence of absence, or rejection or withdrawal in the same way that the silence of God surrounding the Cross of Christ was not a silence of absence or rejection or withdrawal. Instead, in both instances we are faced and challenged by the silence of God that allows human freedom to run its deadly course.

These introductory remarks about the revelation of a suffering God in the cross will only make full sense if we keep in mind John's statement that God is Love. If Love is to express itself in our world and to communicate itself redemptively to others in history, it is difficult to see how Love can avoid pain and suffering. Is not the entry of infinite Love into finite reality itself not only a constraint on the freedom of God but also a limitation that leads to divine suffering, given the rejection of that Love in history? It is difficult for us today to understand a love that is not capable of some form of empathy, sympathy and suffering. From a purely human point of view, a love that does not suffer is somehow something less than love. It was this kind of love, the love that suffers out of love, that was revealed in the passion and death of Jesus on the cross.

Further, these initial reflections on the revelation of the suffering love of God in Christ on the cross will only receive serious consideration if we realise that the contemporary debate about suffering in God is by no means an exclusively twentieth-century issue – even though it seems that suffering in the twentieth-century is a question more troubling for theology than in former centuries. There was a similar debate about suffering in God in the sixth century AD that is worth mentioning here, even though this debate seems to have got lost in classical theology.[22] In the decades after the Council of Chalcedon (451) there persisted, in spite of the clear

21 E. Wiesel. *Night.* London: Penguin Books, 1981, pp. 76-77.
22 A thumbnail sketch of this debate is given by B. Brinkman, 'The Cross in Question' in *To the Lengths of God*, London: Sheed and Ward, 1988, pp. 137-138.

teaching of that Council on the humanity of Jesus, a tendency towards monophysitism. Within this context, Peter the Fuller, Patriarch at Antioch, added to the Good Friday reproaches, O Holy God, the words 'crucified for us'. This in turn was modified by Scythian monks who suggested the formula 'one of the Trinity suffered for us'. In 520 this formula was condemned by Pope Hormisdas, mainly, it would seem, to avoid the possibility of giving a monophysitic interpretation to the formula of the monks. Some years later it became clear that the formula need not be understood as favouring monophysitism. Consequently in 534 Pope John II, in a letter to the Senate at Constantinople, pointed out that the 'one' in the formula refers to 'one person' of the Trinity who has suffered in the flesh.[23] This fascinating exchange in the sixth century shows us something of the struggle that was going on at that time to come to grips, even in a Greek conceptuality, with the suffering of God revealed in the cross of Christ.

In addition, it should be noted that the suffering of God in creation, in Judaism and in the cross of Christ that we have been discussing is not quite the same as the suffering of humanity; it is a suffering only by analogy with human suffering. The crucial difference between the suffering of God and the suffering of humanity is that divine suffering derives from the generosity, fullness and perfection of love in God whereas human suffering derives from a defect of love within the human condition. God suffers in the world and on the cross of Christ out of the abundance of the love of God for the world. God does not suffer in the world out of some need or deficiency within the life of God; instead God suffers in virtue of the overflowing love of God. In contrast, human beings suffer as a result of their finiteness and sinfulness.

Further, it must be pointed out that when we say God suffers we must also insist that God suffers only in order to redeem the

23 The full text of John II is worth quoting here. 'Did Christ our God who in his divinity is impassible, suffer in the flesh?...Christ is one of the holy Trinity, that is, one holy person or subsistence (*subsistentia*) – one *Hypostasis* as the Greeks say – among the three persons of the holy Trinity. The fact that God did truly suffer in the flesh we confirm likewise by the following witnesses (Deut 28:66; Jn 14:6; Mal 3:8; Acts 3:15; 20-28; 1 Cor 2:8; Cyril of Alexandria, Anathematism 12; Leo 1, Tome to Flavian, etc.)'. *The Christian Faith*, J. Neuner and J. Dupuis (eds.). London: Collins, 1983, pp. 155-156.

suffering of humanity. It is not enough simply to say that God suffers, just as we say, for example, that humanity suffers. If this were the case, then we would be left with the abiding question of suffering. Instead, the suffering of God in the world, which arises from the freedom of human beings and their sufferings, is a healing and redemptive suffering. Daniel D. Williams sums up the spirit of these two observations in the following words:

> We miss what is involved in the question about God's suffering if we think primarily of physical pain, mental torment, or death. These are forms of human suffering, to be sure. In Christ, God has in some way experienced them. But 'suffering' has a broader meaning. It signifies to undergo, to be acted upon, to live in a give and take with others. To say that God suffers means that he is actively engaged in dealing with a history which is real to him. What happens makes a difference to him. He wins an actual victory over the world which endures and forgives. It means that the world's sorrow and agony are real to God, indeed in one way more real to him than to us, for only an infinite love can enter completely into sympathetic union with all life.[24]

Unless these fundamental differences between divine and human suffering are kept in mind, the suggestion that God suffers is in danger of being greatly misunderstood.

A Theology of the Darkness of the Cross

What is perhaps equally staggering and shocking about the cross of Christ is that the revelation of God to humanity should take place in such darkness. From a purely human point of view we tend to associate the presence of God in the world with positive experiences of light and life. As such we dissociate the divine from the negative realities of darkness and death.

There is a well known story about the individual who had a little too much to drink one evening and who found himself crawling around on all fours under a street lamp at a corner. When asked by the passing policeman what he was doing, he replied he was searching for the keys of his car which he had lost at the other end

24 Daniel D. Williams, *What Present-Day Theologians are Thinking*, New York: Harper, 1952.

of the street! The policeman then enquired why he was not looking for the keys where he had lost them. The individual replied, 'You see, there's more light up here around this corner'! Many of us tend to look for God in places only where there is light. Yet, as we have already seen in Paul, the cross requires a different kind of human perception, an altogether new way of looking at the world and the mystery of God. This new perspective on God in the world provided by the cross is captured in the words of the German poet Theodore Roethke:

> In a dark time
> The eye begins to see.

The cross of Christ was indeed a dark time and the disciples did begin to see something new about God in the darkness of Calvary. There is a sense in which it can be said with the poet that 'darkness is a special kind of light' (P. Heskith). Matthew tells us that from the sixth to the ninth hour darkness descended on the world (Mt 27:45). The apocalyptic darkness surrounding the cross of Christ is a special kind of light encompassing the Mystery of God in our world. The psalmist reminds us that Yahweh 'made darkness his covering around him, his canopy thick clouds dark with water' (Ps 18:11), and according to the first book of Kings 'The Lord...has said he would dwell in thick darkness' (1 K 8:12). Struggling with the Mystery of God surely includes some experience of darkness. That darkness is at least bearable in the view of the cross of Christ and it can sometimes even be turned into a special kind of light.

A recent playwright sums up the modern mood and experience of humanity with the following words issuing from a beleaguered psychiatrist:

> I need...a way of seeing in the dark.[25]

The world and the Church today need a way to see in the dark, especially a world threatened by the darkness of human, ecological and nuclear holocausts. The cross of Christ provides us with a way of seeing in the dark, not in terms of blindly accepting the darkness but in terms of struggling with the God of Jesus against the human

25 P. Schaffer, *Equus*, New York, 1974, p. 125.

forces of darkness. It was this struggle with the darkness that prompted Martin Luther to say that the christian is someone, who in the face of darkness and death, goes into the garden of life to plant a tree and knows that he or she does not plant in vain.

The darkness of the cross of Christ has many points of contact with our contemporary experience of darkness. One example is the way the darkness of Calvary is re-presented in the darkness surrounding Auschwitz. In both events, there is the complicity of religious groupings. Likewise, both events disclose the potential within humanity and religion for destruction and therefore stand out as warnings for the future. At the same time the revelatory darkness of the cross, 'that special kind of light', may help us to bear the awful memory of Auschwitz without, however, explaining it away or fully understanding it.

At another level Brendan Kennelly's poem about the 'Willow' in the storm captures symbolically something of the powerful way in which the experience of darkness can transform our understanding of life.[26] There are two parts to this poem. The first part describes a storm raging around the Willow:

> But last night that great form
> Was tossed and hit
> By what seemed to me
> A kind of cosmic hate,
> An infernal desire
> To harass and confuse
> Mangle and bewilder.

Out of that terrible storm, there comes a new kind of peace and stillness which is experienced in a special way by the branches of the willow. The second part of the poem describes this new vitality. Before the storm the branches had lived by 'roots...Lodged in apathetic clay' but now after the storm the branches, having felt 'the transfiguring breath of evil', realise

> That what a storm can do
> Is to terrify my roots
> And make me new.

26 B. Kennelly, "Willow".

The scandal of the cross shakes the roots by which we live our lives lodged in apathetic clay. On the one hand the cross reveals the dark side of history, disclosing the enormous potential for evil that is latent in all of us individually and collectively – a kind of cosmic hatred. On the other hand by allowing 'the transfiguring breath of evil', depicted at Calvary to shake our lives once again, we can begin to experience the power of the cross

> To terrify my roots
> And make me new.

The cross of Christ as past historical event and present memory kept alive is a kind of 'sacrament of darkness' enabling us to live with hope in the dark and even sometimes to see beyond the darkness of life. Equally the cross is a kind of 'sacrament of darkness' revealing at one and the same time the depths to which humanity can descend in its orientation towards destruction and the heights to which God can soar in God's capacity to redeem.

Other Dimensions of the Cross

There are of course other aspects to a theology of the cross that can only be mentioned here in passing. Foremost among these is the theology of Mark (Mk 8:34) and Peter (1 P 2:19-25) who present the suffering and death of Christ as a paradigm of christian discipleship. To be a disciple of Christ inevitably involves sharing in the cross of Christ. Christian existence entails the experience of carrying the cross. In saying this, great care must be taken not to give the impression that the christian is someone who must passively accept and endure the cross in a kind of fatalistic patience. The cross is never an end in itself, nor should the cross become an excuse for accepting unjust situations. Instead, the cross in the life of Jesus and in christian existence is a creative moment on the way to newness of life. The blind acceptance of suffering as an end in itself is not the true stuff of christian discipleship. Instead, discipleship of Christ commands the individual to work against suffering and death-dealing forces in our world. For the christian the only adequate response to suffering and death is to do something (praxis) about these negative experiences.

A second aspect to a theology of the cross that should be mentioned here concerns the Reign of God. The form in which the Reign of God is coming to our world is the form of the cross.[27] Entry into the coming Reign of God requires a reversal of values and a new kind of human perception. The change – conversion – is described by Jesus as a rebirth and by the early Church as a process of personal dying and rising. Further, the struggle to advance the Reign of God in our world involves a continuation of that initial dying and rising. Action for justice on behalf of the Reign of God demands a certain letting go of the old and a passing over to the new. This paschal movement at the point of entry into the Reign of God, and throughout life in the struggle to advance the Reign of God, is best understood in terms of a theology of the cross. In both instances the cross is understood not as an end but as a creative means in promoting the coming Reign of God.

A third aspect to the cross that must at least be alluded to here is the contribution of the Gospel of John. According to John, the crucifixion is the moment of glorification. Darkness and light, the lifting up of Christ on the cross and the drawing of humanity to Christ (Jn 12:32) coincide. For John, Christ on the cross is the source of new life – symbolised by the blood and water pouring forth from the side of the crucified Christ.

By way of conclusion it must be said that if this emphasis on the centrality of the cross is not to the fore in our presentation of the gospel, then the message of christianity is in danger of appearing superficially inflated and/or out of touch with the experience of humanity. The experience of the cross in one form or another is a universal human experience with which all can identify. We can begin to talk about salvation in Christ only after we have acknowledged the experience of the estrangement of the self from God and the world. Likewise, if we are to talk about the resurrection we must begin with the experience of the cross. In this way we will discover that resurrection is an experience that is

27 J. Moltmann, *The Crucified God*, op. cit. p. 185.

prefigured in this life, as we shall see in chapter 4. In associating the promise of resurrection with our present experience of the cross, we are suggesting that talk about resurrection becomes more meaningful in so far as it is grounded in present experience. Without some point of contact with present experience, resurrection will appear simply as an addendum to death at the end of this life. When this happens the unity of the death and resurrection of Jesus is once again destroyed. By recovering a theology of the cross it may be possible to safeguard the creative unity that belongs to the saving death and resurrection of Jesus.

4

The Resurrection of Jesus as Gift

The doctrine of the resurrection has been in the news over the last few years, this time as the result of the outspoken Anglican Bishop of Durham, Dr David Jenkins, who tried in 1984 and again in 1989 to provoke people into thinking seriously about the meaning of the resurrection of Jesus. The media moved in quickly on both occasions, summarising Jenkins with one-liners like 'Bishop denies Resurrection'. While it is true that some of Bishop Jenkins' remarks on the resurrection were open to misunderstanding, it must also be pointed out that it was not his intention to deny the resurrection of Jesus as such. One curious result of what has come to be known as the 'Durham Phenomenon'[1] was that the British newspapers editorialised on the Easter Sundays of these two years about the centrality of the resurrection to christian faith, something of a rare event in British journalism.

David Jenkins was trying to communicate to the public some of the fruits of modern biblical and theological thinking on the resurrection in this century, a hazardous task for anyone at the best of times. Yet if the resurrection of Jesus from the dead is central to christian identity, then it is imperative, whatever the risks of

---

1 See T. Harrison, *The Durham Phenomenon*, London: Darton, Longman and Todd, 1985. This book summarises the debate surrounding Bishop Jenkins' views on the resurrection and provides access by way of documentation to what he really said in 1984. A less than careful editorial in *The Tablet*, 8 April 1989 entitled 'A Bishop Who Needs to Think Again' provoked a flurry of correspondence in that journal which captures some of the complex issues involved in discussions about the resurrection.

misunderstanding and misrepresentation by others, that we deepen our 'faith-seeking-understanding' of this central mystery. The Durham Phenomenon and the surrounding publicity at least put people on notice that there may be more to the resurrection of Jesus than they learned at school.

Indeed the resurrection of Jesus from the dead has been the subject of intense biblical research in Catholic circles for the last thirty years. Full book-length studies continue to pour forth from publishing houses, the most recent ones being P. Perkins, *Resurrection: New Testament Witness and Contemporary Reflection* (1984), G. O'Collins, *Jesus Risen* (1987), D. Groegan, *The Death and Resurrection of Jesus* (1988), and G. O'Collins, *Interpreting the Resurrection* (1988).[2]

The purpose of this chapter is not to review critically the available literature but rather to summarise some of the emerging emphases. Attention will be focused on an understanding of the New Testament data and the possibility of developing a contemporary theology of the resurrection of Jesus. The approach throughout will be experiential and hermeneutical.

Finding a Point of Departure

In the pre 1960s most approaches to the resurrection were apologetical. They set out to demonstrate the resurrection as *the* miracle of history which proved objectively the divinity of Jesus.[3] By way of reaction a strongly historical-critical approach was adopted.

2 The number of articles and chapters in books on the resurrection are legion. Some of the more notable ones include W.D. Loewe, 'The Appearances of the Risen Lord: Faith, Fact and Objectivity'. *Horizons* 6 (1979) 177-192, J.P. Galvin, 'The Resurrection of Jesus in Catholic Systematics', *Heythrop Journal* XX (1979) 123-145, and 'The Origin of Faith in the Resurrection of Jesus: Two Recent Perspectives', *Theological Studies* 49 (1988) 25-44; E.A. Johnston, 'Resurrection and Reality in W. Pannenberg', *Heythrop Journal* XXIV (1983) 1-18, F.S. Fiorenza, 'A Reconstructive Hermeneutic of Jesus' Resurrection' *Foundational Theology:* Jesus and the Church, New York: Crossroad, 1984, pp. 29-55; W.P. Thompson, 'The Easter Experiences', *The Jesus Debate: A Survey and Synthesis*, New York: Paulist Press, 1985, pp. 220-247, E. Bredin, 'Reading the Easter Narratives' *Disturbing the Peace: The Way of Discipleship*, Dublin: Columba Press, 1985, pp. 244-260; J.P. Mackey, 'The Way (ii); The Truth that is Done', *Modern Theology: A Sense of Direction*, Oxford: Oxford University Press, 1987, pp. 63-95.

3 The historical background to this approach, especially as it relates by way of response to the enlightenment, is helpfully outlined by F.S. Fiorenza in *Foundational Theology*, Ch. 1.

While this had some advantages, it tended to isolate the experience and language of resurrection from other equally important religious experiences (e.g. Old Testament theophanies) and languages (e.g. exaltation) in the Bible. To overcome these and other defects the historical-critical method is now complemented by a literary-critical approach which attends to the value of the text in itself, focusing on the close relationship that obtains between different literary forms and their revelatory content. A further problem that needs attention in any approach to the resurrection of Jesus is the danger of removing the experience of the resurrection of Jesus in the early Church from the other important, subsequent experiences of the risen Jesus in the christian community.

From the outset it is necessary to stress that some kind of critical correlation between the biblical tradition of resurrection and contemporary experience must be seen to take place. Unless this happens the resurrection of Jesus will come across as just another abstraction in the history of ideas. Of course, mention of the word experience, especially in reference to the resurrection, carries with it a certain ambiguity and so we need to be clear initially what we mean by experience and the interpretation of experience (hermeneutics).

In talking about experience we are proposing something more than simply sense experience; instead we intend that kind of experience which includes critical reflection on the interaction that takes place between a conscious subject and reality, which in turn issues in understanding and interpretation. Further, it must be noted that there is no such thing as a chemically pure, non-interpretative, non-linguistic experience. Experience is only available in and through our interpretations, and our interpretations are available only in and through the language we use.[4] In the specific areas of religious experience it must be stated that the religious dimension of experience is a reality co-present within human experience. In this respect some theologians talk about the religious dimension as something 'co-given'[5]

4 D. Tracy, *Plurality and Ambiguity: Hermeneutics, Religion, Hope*, San Francisco: Harper & Row, 1987, Ch. 3.
5 W. Pannenberg, *Theology and the Philosophy of Science*, London: Darton, Longman and Todd, 1976, p. 301.

and 'co-known'[6] in our experience of the world, while others talk about the 'mediated immediacy'[7] of the divine within the human. The important point here is that we do not normally experience the divine without the medium of finite knowledge, language and reality. In addition, we should remember that every religious experience contains a transcendent dimension that can never be fully captured in our limited interpretations and this dimension is usually referred to as the 'surplus of meaning' which is a basic characteristic of religious experiences. In other words, the revelation that takes place in religious experience is simultaneously one of disclosure and concealment. A final introductory point is that the interpretation of experience is never neutral or disinterested. Every approach to a text or tradition is 'coloured' by the experiences and pre-understandings of the one approaching the text or tradition. This latter principle is particularly true of the person who claims to be detached in his or her approach, a claim which is of course itself a specific and committed point of view. Thus, the critical correlation that should take place between the biblical tradition of resurrection and contemporary experience can be helpfully understood in terms of 'a conversation' (D. Tracy). Within this conversation there will be a 'to-ing' and 'fro-ing' between the text of tradition and the experience of the person approaching the text. The most fruitful conversations in life are those in which each participant respects the other, is able to enter into the concerns of the other, and is prepared to allow these concerns of the other to affect the self. When this begins to happen a fusion of two different horizons takes place that will guide, enrich and correct the two parties in the conversation, in this instance, tradition and experience. In approaching the mystery of the resurrection along these lines it is hoped that we will be able to avoid the extremes of a dogmatism that clings to the past and a relativism that courts only the present.

6   K. Rahner, *Foundations of Christian Faith*, London: Darton, Longman and Todd, 1978, pp. 18-21.
7   E. Schillebeeckx, *Christ: The Christian Experience in the Modern World*, London: SCM Press, 1980, p. 814. cf. also K. Rahner, op.cit. p. 83.

The New Testament Tradition on the Resurrection of Jesus

When we turn to the New Testament evidence on the resurrection of Jesus, we find the existence of two different literary traditions. On the one hand you have what commentators call the early, short *resurrection kerygmata* (proclamations) and on the other hand you have the later, longer *resurrection narratives* (stories) of the gospels.

The resurrection kerygmata are made up of short creedal statements which proclaim the resurrection of Jesus. Examples of these would include: 'God (the Father) raised him from the dead' (Ga 1:1; Ep 1:20; Col 2:12; 1 P 1:21); 'God exalted him' (Ph 2:9; Ac 2:33; 5:31); 'He was ... taken up in glory' (1 Tm 3:16; Jn 17:1-5; Lk 24:26); 'This Jesus you crucified ... God raised him up' (Ac 2:23-24); 'Christ died ... he was raised on the third day ... he appeared' (1 Co 15:3-4); 'The Lord has risen ... and has appeared to Simon' (Lk 24:34); 'Christ died and lived again' (Rm 14:9; 2 Co 13:4); 'He ascended' (Ep 4:7-10; Jn 20:17; Ac 1:9-11); 'He (Jesus) breathed on them and said: "Receive the holy spirit"' (Jn 20:22; Ac 2:1-4).

Alongside these short creedal statements you have the longer resurrection narratives of the gospels. These resurrection narratives cover the appearance-traditions and the empty tomb tradition. The appearance tradition may be classified according to geographical location with accounts in Galilee (Mt 28; Jn 21; Mk 16:1-8) and accounts in Jerusalem (Lk 24; Jn 20; Mk 16:9-20). Another possible classification is that of appearances to assembled groups (the twelve, five hundred) and appearances to particular individuals (Peter, Mary Magdalen, James, Paul). While these appearance-narratives differ in historical detail, they all cohere substantially in describing a real encounter with Jesus as living and personally present to his disciples after his death.

Concerning the empty tomb tradition there is considerable disagreement among commentators. Some see it as a late legendary elaboration of the resurrection, developed for apologetic reasons; others hold that it contains a reliable historical core. The latter view seems to be the more plausible in view of the presence of female witnesses in a culture that normally would not invoke female witnesses as reliable evidence, and in virtue of the impossibility of proclaiming the tomb to be empty if in fact it was intact.

Interpreting the New Testament Tradition

How are we today to interpret this schematic summary of the literary tradition about the resurrection of Jesus from the dead? What is the import of the wide variety of language and testimony given in the resurrection kerygmata and narratives? Is there any point of contact between the experiences of the first disciples and the experiences that contemporary christians have of the risen Jesus? Is a fusion of horizons possible between biblical tradition and contemporary experience?

To begin to answer these questions a preliminary observation must be made. We cannot come cold and neutral from the outside to the New Testament evidence and expect to understand it. A minimum requirement would demand that we approach the resurrection data from within a position of basic, Jewish faith. This would involve at least a disposition of personal openness and receptivity to the experience of God in the world, a recognition of the existence of different theophanies (encounters with Yahweh) in the course of Jewish history, and a fascination with the preaching, praxis and death of Jesus. Likewise it would be necessary to have some sense of basic, Jewish hope. The hope in question here includes the universal hope belonging to the human condition which finds partial expression at least in the later Jewish hope of a general resurrection of the dead at the end of time. Without these predispositions, it would be difficult to enter into any real conversation with the New Testament evidence on the resurrection.

Assuming this minimum we can now begin to interact with the New Testament story of the resurrection. One possible explanation of the evidence is the suggestion that the resurrection accounts are simply an interpretation of the life and death of Jesus. It is proposed by some that after the death of Jesus the disciples came together around the camp fire, reflected on the life of Jesus, and concluded through an upsurge of enthusiasm and insight that the work of Jesus must go on. This enthusiasm and insight is expressed and communicated in different literary accounts of the resurrection. For example, Rudolph Bultmann holds that Jesus rose in the kerygma of the early Church[8] and Willie Marxsen claims that the resurrection accounts are ways of saying that the cause of Jesus must continue in the world today.[9] The difficulty with these and similar theories is that they fail to explain adequately what, given the scandal of the death of Jesus, triggered off this response to the life of Jesus. Equally, they do not account for the dramatic recovery and renewal of faith in the followers of Jesus as well as a significant change of vision and praxis in the lives of the frightened disciples. Likewise, there is insufficient conceptual and theological precedent within Judaism, especially in terms of positing the resurrection of an individual as the dawning of the end of time, to justify this kind of consistent interpretation of the life and death of Jesus. Is not the theological load we normally associate with the doctrine of the resurrection, such as Spirit, Salvation, Church, eucharist and eschatology, simply too heavy to place on the shoulders of unaided reflection on the life and death of Jesus? Surely new beginnings after the death of Jesus require new experiences and interpretations. It is these perspectives that we would like to explore further as a key to understanding the literary accounts of the resurrection kerygmata and narratives.

The basic thesis we wish to propose is that after the crucifixion the disciples had new experiences of Jesus, that these post-crucifixion experiences gave rise to a new understanding and interpretation of Jesus, and that this new vision of Jesus is expressed in the resurrection kerygmata and narratives. By reflecting on the life, teaching, praxis, death and post-Calvary experiences, the disciples came to see/understand/interpret/know Jesus and themselves in a new way. This new and changed perception of Jesus and themselves is conveyed to us in the resurrection kerygmata and narratives.

8   R. Bultmann, 'The New Testament and Mythology', *Kerygma and Myth*, H.W. Bartsch (ed.), New York: Harper & Row, 1961, pp. 41-42.
9   W. Marxsen, *The Resurrection of Jesus of Nazareth*, London: SCM Press, 1970, pp. 83-84.

In the resurrection kerygmata there is, as we have seen above, a great variety of linguistic expression. This includes resurrection, exaltation, ascension, glorification, living again and Pentecost. These models are different attempts to come to grips with the personal experience of Jesus after his death on the cross. The variety of language within the early Church's proclamation captures some of the intensity and richness of these new, ongoing, dramatic, post-crucifixion experiences of Jesus by the first disciples. Further, this variety of language also points towards the 'surplus of meaning' that belongs to the disciples' experience of the crucified and risen Jesus.

Is it possible to discover the original and primary model describing the resurrection kerygmata after the death of Jesus? To date, it is extremely difficult to get agreement among commentators as to the oldest form of the christian articulation of the experience of Jesus after his death. Some argue that the one-verse resurrection formula, God raised Jesus from the dead, is the earliest.[10] Others, however, claim that the language of exaltation is primary or that the resurrection was simply one among many models in the very early Church describing the experience of Jesus after his death.[11] What does seem clear, however, is that the language of resurrection predominates very early on and that the symbolism of death and resurrection moves quickly to the centre of the christian proclamation. The reasons why the motif of resurrection become so central to the gospel proclamation are complex.

In general terms the symbol of personal resurrection from the dead resonates with the human experience of hope for life beyond death that is intrinsic to the human condition. In more specific Judaic terms, the resurrection of Jesus confirms the christ-ology/soteriology implicit in the preaching and praxis of Jesus; it

10 See the helpful summary and defence of this point of view given by F. Fiorenza, *Foundational Theology*, pp. 33-37, and the bibliography supporting this position on p. 53 n.114. W.M. Thompson in *The Jesus Debate*, pp. 220-223, discusses this question and inclines also towards the view of resurrection as the primary model.
11 See X. Léon-Dufour, *Resurrection and the Message of Easter*, London: G. Chapman, 1974, pp. 38-42; E. Schillebeeckx, *Jesus: An Experiment in Christology*, London: Collins, 1979, pp. 403-515; *Interim Report*, London: SCM Press, 1980, pp. 74-93; P. Perkins, *Resurrection*, 1984, p. 20; J.A. Fitzmyer, 'The Ascension of Christ and Pentecost' *Theological Studies* 45 (1984) 409-440; E. Bredin, *Disturbing the Peace*, 1985, op. cit. ch. X.

also captures the eschatological character of the post-crucifixion experience of Jesus. Here it should be kept in mind that the general resurrection of the dead is associated in Judaism with the end of time. Further, the symbol of resurrection sums up what happened to Jesus in death, that is what God did to Jesus in death: exaltation and glorification. In addition, the symbol of resurrection expresses the full identity of Jesus: Jesus of Nazareth is now the exalted Lord, sitting at the right hand of God the Father. Lastly, the resurrection symbolises the advent of the Reign of God into our world in the person of Jesus.

Thus when we begin to reflect on the symbol of resurrection, we find ourselves drawing on other models of the resurrection kerygmata: exaltation, glorification, ascension and Pentecost. The language of resurrection alone is insufficient to understand the resurrection kerygmata of the early Church. Recourse must be had to the other models 'which have the function of correcting and complementing the vocabulary of resurrection'.[12] In particular, if we are to avoid a literalist understanding of the resurrection that would reduce it merely to a physical resuscitation then we must invoke the complementary, more expansive and less materialist language of exaltation, glorification, ascension and Pentecost.

Turning to the resurrection narratives of the appearances it is quite clear that we are dealing with much later accounts of post-crucifixion experiences of Jesus. This observation, however, does not entitle us to hold that the appearances are merely creations of the early Church. Instead, the appearances are the outcome, to be sure the developed outcome, of real, historical, personal experiences of Jesus after his death. The appearances contain a historical core, even though many of them may have undergone several different redactions. An obvious example of this redactional development is the story of the appearance of the risen Jesus to the two disciples on the road to Emmaus (Lk 24). Thus, the different accounts of the appearances are amplified stories, describing the personal encounters of the first disciples with Jesus after his death.

---

12 C. Geffré, 'The Resurrection of Christ as an Interpretative Testimony', *The Risk of Interpretation,* New York: Paulist Press, 1987, p. 88.

Rather than suggest that the appearances are simply colourful elaborations of the resurrection kerygmata, it seems more appropriate to hold that the appearances are an additional model alongside the other models describing what happened to Jesus. Whereas the resurrection kerygmata tend to tell us what God did to Jesus, most of the appearance-narratives with some exceptions spell out for us the effects of the resurrection of Jesus on the disciples. To this extent, the appearances are best understood in relationship to the other models of resurrection, exaltation, glorification, living again, ascension and Pentecost. Within this context the appearance stories fulfil several important theological functions.

First of all the appearances establish an important point of continuity between the historical Jesus and the early christian communities. Secondly, they describe the coming to be and full recognition of Jesus as the Christ who is the exalted Lord, the Son of God incarnate. Thirdly, by including women as recipients, the appearance stories are an important testimony to the establishment in a culture of patriarchy of a new discipleship of equality among women and men called and commissioned to proclaim the resurrection at the very origins of the christian movement. Fourthly, the appearances establish an intrinsic connection between the resurrection and the foundation of the Church. As J. Sobrino states: 'The Church is ... an integral and essential part of ... Christ's resurrection'.[13] Fifthly, the appearances legitimate the universal mission and ministry of the disciples in the world. Sixthly, the appearances point up the eucharist as the primary mode of access to the risen Christ for the followers of Jesus. Lastly, the appearances show that the resurrection is also about ascension into heaven and the outpouring of the Spirit of Christ upon the first disciples. This ascension of Christ and the outpouring of the Spirit are not events that come only forty days (Ac 1:1-11) or fifty days (Ac 2:1-4) after the death of Jesus. Rather these are also events that are portrayed as having happened on Easter Sunday morning (Lk 24:50-51; Mk 16:19; Jn 20:19-23).[14] As P. Benoit put it so well some thirty years ago,

13   J. Sobrino, *The True Church and the Poor*, London: SCM Press, 1985, p. 87.
14   See J.A. Fitzmyer, art.cit.

while there are different phases to the glorification of Christ in regard to our understanding *(quoad nos),* there is one event as such for Christ *(quoad Christum).*[15] In coming to grips with the profound significance of the Easter-event the early Church had no difficulty in uniting the historical and the theological.

If we are to tell the full story of what happened after the crucifixion to Jesus and to his disciples, then reference must be made to all the models: exaltation, resurrection, glorification, living again, ascension, Pentecost and appearances. Further, if the full meaning of the resurrection of Jesus is to be recovered and safeguarded from literalist distortions, then a formal account of the other complementary models of exaltation, glorification, ascension and Pentecost must be taken into consideration. No one model is sufficient in itself to describe the whole experience and yet it has to be said that the fullness of this experience is greater than the sum of the individual models.

Focusing on the Experiences in the Interpretations

Clearly, it is impossible for us today to recover the original experiences of the first disciples. These foundational experiences, embedded in the different interpretations, are available only in the testimony of the resurrection kerygmata and narratives. Does this mean that the original experiences of Jesus after his death are beyond all recovery from a contemporary point of view? More specifically, must we say that what took place after the death of Jesus was so unique that it no longer takes place today?

One school of thought seems to suggest that what happened after the death of Jesus is absolutely unique, quite specific to that period, and therefore exclusive and unrepeatable. This outlook posits a break between the experience of the first disciples and the experiences of contemporary christians. The underlying emphasis here is one of discontinuity between past and present experiences. Another school of thought suggests that there is no radical difference between the experiences of the first disciples and contemporary experience. Within this school the emphasis is on the

15 P. Benoit, *Exégèse et théologie*, Paris: Le Cerf, 1961, pp. 402-404.

underlying continuity between past and present experience so that what takes place today parallels what took place two thousand years ago. Are these two points of view incompatible and irreconcilable? Is there not some retrievable truth in both schools?

To deal with this question we must attend more closely to the original experience contained in the literary evidence of the resurrection kerygmata and narratives. There are at least two qualities belonging to the original experience by the disciples of Jesus after his death on the cross that are worth exploring, namely the existence of a new mode of presence of Jesus to the disciples after his death and the association of this new presence with the end of time *(eschaton)*.

The experiences that the disciples had after the crucifixion are initiated and sustained by this new personal presence of Jesus. After his death on the cross, Jesus is experienced as a new presence and power, personally alive and active in the lives of the disciples, a presence that transforms and assembles the disciples for the purpose of creating a new people, missioning them, and holding them together in and through the one Spirit. It is this new experience of Jesus as personally alive and present to the disciples that is interpreted by them in the resurrection kerygmata and narratives. The variety of models captures one or other element of this new, dynamic and empowering presence. In all instances, it is the personal presence of Jesus that effects the new experiences. This element of personal presence is highlighted especially by the models of living again, appearance and Pentecost.

In addition to the element of personal presence, there is also the element of eschatological disclosure and break-through associated with this new presence, symbolised by the association of this new presence as an event occurring 'on the third day'. The new presence of Jesus is a presence of power in spite of the devastating death of Jesus on the cross and therefore includes a sense of victory and triumph over death as the object of human and Jewish hope. This eschatological dimension of the experience is also brought out symbolically in the models of resurrection, exaltation, glorification and Pentecost. Combining these different interpretations of one and the same experience we are given a picture of Jesus, personally present to the disciples in a new way, who is now perceived as the risen Christ (resurrection and appearances), the exalted Lord (exaltation and ascension) and living Spirit (Pentecost and glorification).

If we can agree that the experience of Jesus after his death includes at least a real sense of Jesus as a new personal power and presence, embodying an eschatological dimension touching the lives of his followers, then it becomes difficult to sustain the thesis of a radical break between the experience of the first disciples and the experiences of contemporary christians. Surely the axis of christian faith is about affirming the reigning presence of the historical Jesus as a new reality and Spirit in the world and the christian community. To this extent we must insist on some continuity between the experiences of the first disciples and our experience of Jesus today. Thus we find Rahner cautioning us: 'We ourselves do not stand simply and absolutely outside the experience of the apostolic witness'.[16] Instead, Rahner suggests two basic points of contact between the experiences of the first disciples and ourselves today. There is first of all our primordial experience of hope, what Rahner calls 'our transcendental hope in resurrection' which the first disciples would have had and which would have been a factor enabling them to be open and receptive to the resurrection of Jesus. There is also our experience of the Spirit of the risen Christ today in the christian community. According to Rahner: 'We ourselves experience the resurrection of Jesus in the 'Spirit' because we experience him and his "cause" as living and victorious'.[17] Having clearly established this continuity between the experience of the first disciples and our experience of Jesus today, it is important, nonetheless, to acknowledge that there is an aspect to the experience of the first disciples that is unique and unrepeatable. First of all, the experiences of the early disciples establish a unity between the new experiences of the post-crucified Jesus and the

16 K. Rahner, *Foundations of Christian Faith*, p. 275.
17 Ibid. Though Rahner's language here is slightly reminiscent of Marxsen, Rahner's position is quite distinct and different from that of Marxsen.

historical Jesus in a way that no other subsequent generation could. The first disciples had known the earthly Jesus and were the only ones who could establish an identity between the earthly Jesus and the post-crucified risen Jesus, now powerfully present as Spirit. Secondly, the interpretation of these new experiences of Jesus after his death in terms of resurrection, exaltation, glorification, living again, ascension and Pentecost is normative for all subsequent generations. The manner and mode of this new presence of the personal and victorious Spirit of Jesus is laid down in these models for later christians. Thus, it is only in virtue of this apostolic witness and testimony contained in the New Testament that we today can experience and recognise Jesus, personally present as exalted Lord and active as Spirit in the christian community and the world.

By exaggerating the difference between the experience of the first disciples and the contemporary experience of the Spirit of Jesus, some have unwittingly diminished the importance of the challenge to discern the transforming power and Spirit of Jesus in the Church and the world today. It is ultimately the same Spirit of the risen Jesus that touched the minds and hearts of the first disciples which touches the minds and hearts of christians today. The difference between the early disciples and contemporary christians is that they, the first disciples, were prepared for this new experience of Jesus in and through their personal experience of the life, preaching, praxis and death of Jesus, whereas we today are prepared for this continuing experience of the Spirit of Jesus on the basis of their witness and testimony.

One clue to the mode and manner of the Spirit of the risen Jesus in our world today may be gauged from the appearance-narratives. In many of the appearances the risen Jesus is experienced sacramentally: in the breaking of bread (Lk 24:13-25; Jn 21:1-14), in the forgiveness of sins (Jn 20:21-23), in the communication of the Spirit (Mt 28:16-20; Jn 20:22) and in the experience of conversion symbolised in baptism (Mt 28:19-20). The experience of the appearance of the risen Jesus in these sacramental encounters is significant because it is consistent with the principles outlined earlier for understanding the dynamics of human experience, including the religious experience of resurrection. The credibility of the experience of the risen Jesus both in the past or in the present is not enhanced by suggesting that the original experience is 'the great exception' to the principles operative in subsequent religious experiences. As noted above, we do not experience the divine outside the finite medium of human experience; instead, the religious dimension of human experience is discovered as co-given and co-present in our experiences of finite reality, a claim that reflects the principle of Incarnation as an essential part of the christian reality. Likewise, the experience of the risen Jesus is not an experience of a disembodied Spirit but rather an experience, that is co-given and co-mediated in and through designated sacramental activities. Of course, the new power and presence of the risen Jesus are not confined only to sacramental experiences as we can see from the other appearance-narratives, though the details of this mediating activity are not always clear in some instances. The Spirit of the risen Jesus can also be co-experienced today in the different forms of praxis enunciated by the earthly Jesus that promote the reign of God: caring for the poor, the struggle for justice, visiting the sick, love of neighbour and respecting unconditionally the dignity of every human being.

Fusing the Horizons of Tradition and Contemporary Experience

Having examined and interpreted the New Testament data on resurrection and the experience within that data, we are now in a position to correlate the meaning of resurrection with contemporary human experience. What does the message of resurrection have to say to contemporary experience? What particular human experiences of life today does the resurrection of Jesus express? If we can begin to tackle these questions we may be able to pave the way for a fusion of horizons between the christian tradition of resurrection and contemporary experience. Unless some kind of interaction can take place between tradition and experience there is the danger that the resurrection of Jesus will remain a dead dogma of the past. A sample of contemporary experiences pertinent to these questions would include the experiences of fragmentation, injustice and death, and the future.

A. Fragmentation: The words of the Irish poet W.B. Yeats, 'Things fall apart, the centre cannot hold', sum up the experience of many people today. As we move historically through epochal changes and paradigm shifts, we experience a deep sense of brokenness between the past and the present, between the old and the new, between the dead and the living. These experiences find expression for some in the so-called 'break-down of traditional values' and for others in the growing insecurity about the future. A further symptom of this fragmentation can be found in the disturbing divorce between humanity and nature as well as the dangerous split between spirit and matter. The mechanisation of nature and the technological control of society are contributing to a new kind of human loneliness and isolation. Due to this fragmentation the self as self becomes an ego and less a relational subject, separated from other human subjects, from nature, and from modern technology. The unity of the human race and its history are threatened by this growing sense of fragmentation and human isolation. It is against this background of brokenness and disconnectedness that we hear calls from all quarters for a new sense of solidarity: solidarity between humanity and nature, solidarity between the past and the present, solidarity between the rich and the poor, solidarity among women and men. This call to a new solidarity within the human family is becoming the major premise, the *sine qua non*, of human and planetary survival. Unless a new alliance and solidarity can be forged between nature and humanity, between spirit and matter, between the strong and the weak, scientists and sociologists alike predict a prospect of destruction within the human family. But what is the basis of this call to solidarity, are there any grounds for affirming the fundamental unity of the human race, is there any prospect for regaining 'the lost togetherness' of history, humanity and nature?

Is there not a case to be made that the ultimate source of human solidarity is to be found in God's solidarity with the human enterprise? Can we not say that the resurrection of Jesus is the ultimate act of divine solidarity with humanity and the whole world? In the resurrection, we have God's personal acceptance and adoption of the human condition. A new kind of unity and solidarity is forged in the resurrection of Jesus between God and the world, between spirit and matter. We find Paul expressing something of this solidarity in potent statements like: 'You are all one in Christ' (Gla 3:28) because 'by one Spirit, we were all baptised into the one Body' (1 Co 12:13), so that now 'if one member suffers, all suffer together; if one member is honoured, all rejoice together' (1 Co 12:26). Equally, Paul's rich theology of our baptismal and eucharistic unity 'in Christ' is an application of his understanding of this new solidarity between Christ and humanity. Further, this new principle of humanity's solidarity 'in Christ', based on the resurrection, extends to the whole of creation so that the author of the letter to the Ephesians talks about a plan for the unity of all things in heaven and on earth, taking place in the fullness of time (Ep 1:9-10). The doctrine of the resurrection is a symbol uniting in solidarity God and the world, humanity and nature, matter and spirit in a way that enables us to see beyond the immediate experiences of fragmentation and isolation. In and through the resurrection of Jesus, God has entered into a new oneness with the human race that is the basis of the contemporary call to a universal solidarity embracing past, present and future.

B. Injustice and death: Everyone at some stage in life experiences evil and suffering and, if we are to be honest, we have all contributed directly or indirectly to the quantum of evil and suffering in our world. This pervasiveness of evil and suffering on a global scale is one of the most imponderable questions facing humanity and theology today. While it is true to say that the only adequate response to the question of evil and suffering is to do something about reducing their existence, we know that evil and suffering all too frequently overcome our best-laid plans and efforts at elimination. In turn, evil and suffering generate a world of extraordinary injustices and inequalities. The innocent and the weak are all too often the victims of human, historical and blind forces. The human story is marked by tragedy in its origins and its endings.

To outward appearances, evil and suffering, injustice and inequality, seem to be confirmed in the finality of death. To acknowledge this state of affairs with all honesty and realism is at least to recognise the flawed state of the human condition and its history. In recognising the jagged edges of human existence and the awful ambiguity of living and dying, we begin to understand what it means to hope against hope. Human hopes arise out of a stubborn refusal to give way in the face of so much evil and suffering, out of the extraordinary ability to begin again after being touched by tragedy, out of momentary human glimpses of transcendence in the midst of pain and joy. These hopes, though fragile, are a persistent and universal experience of the human spirit. This common experience raises questions about the validity, endurance and permanence of existence, questions that provide a possible point of contact with the meaning of the resurrection of Jesus.

Within this context the resurrection of Jesus is a kind of divine protest and promise against the apparent emptiness and futility of existence. The symbol of resurrection is an assurance that evil and suffering do not have the last word, that injustice and inequality do not finally endure, that death is not in truth the end. Resurrection reverses the outward appearances of living and dying, and reminds us that invisible realities deep down do count in the long run. Put more positively, the resurrection of Jesus from the dead is a statement that good triumphs over evil, that suffering can be transformed into new life, that justice will take over from injustice, that death itself is a point of entry into newness of life. Resurrection within its Jewish roots was about a divine judgment that gathers up the good, rescues the lost and redeems the brokenness of life. The resurrection of Jesus from the dead is ultimately about the resurrection of our world in life and in death, symbolised in statements by Paul that the risen Jesus 'is the first-born among the dead', 'the first fruits' of God's harvest, and a 'life-giving Spirit' (1 Co 15).

C. The future: A third contemporary experience that might be explored is our experience of the future. For many, too many perhaps, the experience of the future is empty, shapeless, and without any content. This futureless future is summed up in Nietzsche's nihilistic 'myth of the eternal recurrence of the same'. There is no sense of direction, no vision of a future, no possibility of an individual or global destiny. This absence of a future affects the way we see the worthwhileness of the present. Pure transience can reduce the human passion for living and loving. This particular experience of the future is further compounded by the possibility of mass nuclear and ecological destruction. There can be little doubt that the threat of nuclear annihilation on a global scale and more recently the threat of ecological collapse have altered human consciousness and affected its confidence in the future. A vacuous future and destiny diminishes the dignity of the individual, the worthwhileness of existence, and the social significance of life.

The resurrection of Jesus from the dead and its interpretation in the life of the New Testament Church stands out in sharp contrast to this empty contemporary experience of the future. The Easter-event points us towards the future, giving it symbolic shape and content. On the one hand, the resurrection of Jesus provides us with a clue to the real existence of a future after death. The event of resurrection is a counter-claim to the suggestion that death is the definitive end of life and that the future is empty for the individual and society. The experience of the Spirit of Jesus after his death on the cross as personally present, transforming, empowering and missioning people is an assurance that the human enterprise does have a future. The continuing power and presence of the Spirit of Jesus in the world today is likewise a guarantee that the human spirit in death will not simply slip away into nothing. On the other hand the resurrection of Jesus also gives us some intimation about the quality and character of that future. The narrative accounts of appearances and empty tomb suggest that the resurrection is more than simply the immortality of the soul, more than merely a spiritual survival. The appearances and empty tomb imply that resurrection affects spirit *and* matter, humanity *and* creation. The New Testament language of 'first fruits', 'spiritual body', 'new Adam', and 'the new creation' imply change and transformation as well as completion and fulfilment not only for the individual but also for the whole of humanity and creation. When talking about the resurrection of Jesus, therefore, we are talking about the coming into being of something new in history, the holding out of a new promise and hope for those who come after Jesus as well as those who preceded Jesus, and the setting up of a new goal for the whole of humanity, history and creation. The resurrection of Jesus is both a christological and eschatological event. It tells us something about Jesus but also something about our individual, social and cosmic destiny.

Wolfhart Pannenberg, more than most, has developed these perspectives on the resurrection of Jesus from the dead.[18] According to Pannenberg the resurrection of Jesus is an anticipation of the end *(prolepsis)* and as such is, therefore, a disclosure in principle of the future to come. In and through the resurrection of Jesus, the Reign of God has come into existence, a new world has dawned, and reality has been given a radical orientation towards the future.The resurrection of Jesus is the pre-appearance of the end of time, the arrival in outline of the end of the world, giving us a preview as it were of the life to come. To this extent, the resurrection provides us with a new way of looking at life and reality. It lights up the meaning of life and death, gives a new value to individual and social praxis, intimates that human existence and history are on their way to a still outstanding future, and therefore assures us that the world has a destiny and future 'in Christ'. It is Jesus Christ, the crucified but risen and exalted One, who is the form and shape of the world to come. In a word, it is the risen Christ who both fulfils human hopes and in doing so becomes the new ground and object of christian hope.

Concluding Remarks

What begins to emerge from this brief analysis of some contemporary experiences is that there is a point of contact, a

18 See W. Pannenberg, *Jesus – God and Man*, London, SCM Press, 1968, ch. 3; 'The Revelation of God in Jesus of Nazareth', *Theology as History*, J.M. Robinson and J.B. Cobb (eds.), New York: Harper & Row, 1967. For a constructive and impressive review of Pannenberg's thinking on the resurrection see E.A. Johnson, 'Resurrection and Reality in the Thought of W. Pannenberg', *Heythrop Journal* XXIV (1983) 1-18.

possible fusion of horizons, between the tradition of resurrection and contemporary experience. Within this exchange and interaction the symbol of resurrection becomes a way of 're-ordering' our experience and understanding of the world.[19] This process of re-ordering and restructuring our world affects not just intellectual horizons but also, and perhaps more importantly, our practical reason. The promise of resurrection provides a perspective for a new kind of individual and social praxis. What we do and how we act for the sake of the coming reign of God takes on added significance in the light of the resurrection.

W. Pannenberg would have us go further, suggesting that the resurrection of Jesus requires a change in our understanding of reality.[20] From now on reality must be seen as having an eschatological thrust, that is, reality has a radical orientation towards completion and fulfilment in Christ. This enables Pannenberg to construct 'an eschatological ontology': an understanding of the whole of reality coming under the influence of the resurrection of Jesus who is the power and pull of the future upon the present.[21]

Thus the resurrection is about a special kind of knowing and doing; it provides us with a particular vision of life. In the technical discourse of epistemology, the language of resurrection is an imaginative interpretation of existence – based on the historical life, teaching, praxis, death and post-crucifixion experiences of Jesus. Imagination is that particular faculty which provides a key to the interpretation and understanding of human experience. Imagination plays an essential role in all knowing and as such enables us to organise and filter the ordinary experiences of life as meaningful or meaningless.[22] Imagination, therefore, should not, as in much popular usage, be associated with the production of simply the wild and fanciful.

19 The image of resurrection as a way of 're-ordering' life is helpfully proposed by G. O'Collins, *Jesus Risen*, New York: Paulist Press, 1987, pp. 131-145.
20 See E.A. Johnson, art.cit.
21 See B.J. Walsh, 'Pannenberg's Eschatological Ontology', *Christian Scholar's Review* II (1982), 229-249.
22 The place and role of the imagination in epistemology is the subject of an important symposium edited by J.P. Mackey, *Religious Imagination*, Edinburgh: Edinburgh University Press, 1986. See also J. P. Mackey in *Modern Theology*, op. cit. pp.24-30.

What is distinctive about the resurrection as an imaginative key and framework for understanding life is that it focuses on and rediscovers for us today in the twentieth century the unity of the world, the solidarity of the human race, and 'the altogetherness' of creation. This particular perspective of resurrection stands out in opposition to a world imaginatively interpreted and understood in terms of discreet individualism, dualism, and fragmentation.

To conclude these remarks on the relationship between resurrection and experience, it becomes necessary to add a few qualifiers or principles of interpretation that should characterise any theology of the resurrection of Jesus. In talking about the resurrection, we must be careful not to claim too much and equally careful not to be too objectivist in the statements that we make. The essence of the resurrection of Jesus as the ground and object of christian hope is that it should continue to remain open and unqualified at the level of hope. To say too much or to be too clear about the resurrection would be to remove it from the realm of hope. The revelation that takes place in the resurrection of Jesus, like all revelation as we noted earlier, is one of simultaneous disclosure and concealment. The disclosure given in the resurrection of Jesus is enough to enable us to hope in a new key and the concealment that takes place in the resurrection of Jesus is such as to keep us sufficiently searching and expectant in our hope. In other words, a good theology of resurrection must leave room for the elements of surprise and newness.

A second principle governing our understanding of the resurrection is that our best insights about the meaning of resurrection are derived from saying what the resurrection is not. Of course, in saying what the resurrection of Jesus is not, we are beginning to glimpse darkly what it is. For example, by claiming that the resurrection of Jesus *is not simply* a physical resuscitation, nor merely a restoration to life, nor just a picking up of where Jesus left off at death, nor only a spiritual survival, nor solely a continuation of this life, we are beginning 'to see' the real meaning and promise of resurrection.

A third principle that should be kept in mind in talking about the resurrection of Jesus is that care should be taken not to allow such discourse to be used as the easy answer to the existence of so much pain, suffering and death in our world or, even worse, to justify the blind, passive acceptance of evil and injustice. The rhetoric of resurrection must be moderated and qualified by the dark reality of the ongoing presence of the cross of Christ in our world. To this extent the resurrection of Jesus and the hope of resurrection for the world must become a stimulus to a new and creative praxis that refuses resolutely to accept the status quo of so much evil, suffering and injustice in our world. Resurrection is not about 'more of the same'; instead it is about personal change and the transformation of social structures in our world for the sake of the coming reign of God. The resurrection therefore is not solely something that happens after death; it is also something that affects the character of daily life and living *before* death. In a word, the logic of resurrection and the hope it inspires is not the logic of inference but of imagination and new praxis.

5

A Theology of the Paschal Mystery

In our chapter on the cross of Christ we made passing reference to the importance of seeing the death and resurrection of Jesus as a unity. Yet, almost in defiance of that plea we were forced to deal with the cross more or less in isolation from the resurrection. Likewise, when we came to examine the resurrection we did so without much reference to the cross. This was necessary in order to grasp some of the distinctive elements of, respectively, the death and resurrection of Jesus. To overcome this apparent inconsistency we now propose to say something about the death and resurrection as a single saving reality. Our objective here is to outline some of the ingredients of a broadly based theology of the Paschal Mystery. Having looked separately at the life, death, and resurrection of Jesus we are now in a position to see how these realities hold together more properly as a unity.

The Rediscovery of the Paschal Mystery at Vatican II

One of the concepts running through the documents of Vatican II is that of the Paschal Mystery.[1] The work of redemption by Christ is achieved principally by the Paschal Mystery[2]; the norm guiding the revision of the liturgy is the Paschal Mystery[3]; the Church 'proclaims' and 'celebrates' the Paschal Mystery in her liturgical

---

1 *S.C.*, a. 5, 6, 61, 104, 106, 107; *G.S.*, a. 22, 38, 52; *A.G.*, a.14; *O.T.*, a.8.
2 *S.C.*, a. 5.
3 *S.C.*, a. 107; *A.G.*, a. 14.

life;[4] Christians are invited to imitate the Paschal Mystery in their ordinary everyday lives;[5] ministers of the gospel are challenged to live the Paschal Mystery so that they can initiate others into it.[6] The Council broadly describes the Paschal Mystery in terms of the passion, death, resurrection and ascension of our Lord Jesus Christ.[7] Perhaps a more formal account would say that the Paschal Mystery is about the redemptive unity that obtains between the life, death, resurrection, ascension of Jesus Christ and the outpouring of the Holy Spirit. The key elements in the Paschal Mystery are of course the death and resurrection as a single saving reality, but these cannot be fully understood without reference to what has gone before and comes after.

The immediate background to the rediscovery of the Paschal Mystery at Vatican II was the biblical and liturgical renewal that had been sweeping through the Catholic Church since World War II. Prior to this, most theologies of redemption were focused exclusively on the death of Jesus. Theories of expiation, atonement and satisfaction concentrated on the blood-sacrifice of Christ on the cross, white little or no serious attention was given to the resurrection. With the renewal in biblical studies, however, the resurrection of Jesus began to acquire a new importance through the influential works of scholars like F.X. Durwell and D. Stanley.[8] Initially, perhaps, this new emphasis on the resurrection succeeded at the expense of the death of Jesus. The renewed theologies of the cross and the resurrection which we summarised in the last two chapters provide new foundations for working out a theology of the Paschal Mystery.

The rediscovery of the Paschal Mystery at Vatican II has had a profound impact on the liturgical and pastoral life of the Church. It has influenced the renewal of the liturgy of Holy Week and Easter.

---

4   *S.C.*, a. 104.
5   *G.S.*, a. 22, 38, 52.
6   *O.T.*, a. 8.
7   *S.C.*, a. 5, 61.
8   See F.X., Durwell, *The Resurrection: A Biblical Study,* London: Sheed and Ward, 1960; D.M. Stanley, *Christ's Resurrection in Pauline Soteriology,* Rome: Biblical Institute Press, 1961.

While Good Friday still retains its own intrinsic importance, it nonetheless points towards the Easter Vigil. Good Friday is, as it were, the preface to the Easter Vigil; it sets the appropriate atmosphere for the inbreaking of the mystery of the resurrection which is celebrated during the vigil of Holy Saturday night. Likewise, the Paschal Mystery has influenced the structure of the celebration of the sacraments. The Liturgy Constitution of Vatican II mentions specifically the sacraments of Baptism and Eucharist as celebrations of the Paschal Mystery[9] and suggests that the funeral service should reflect 'the Paschal character of christian death'.[10] The language of the Paschal Mystery is prominent in the liturgical life of the christian community. The prefaces and prayers of both Lent and Easter refer quite frequently to the Paschal Mystery.

The word 'paschal' comes from the Greek term, *pascha*, which goes back to the Hebrew, *pesach,* which refers to the annual commemoration by the Israelites of their liberating passover from slavery in Egypt. The Paschal Mystery is intended to pick up for christians this rich Hebrew background and to locate the historical death and resurrection of Jesus as the establishment of a new liberating passover. According to John's Gospel the death of Jesus takes place on the same day as the Jews were celebrating the Passover and offering sacrifice in the temple. St Paul tells us that 'Christ, our Paschal Lamb, is sacrificed, (1 Co 5:7). This paralleling of the death and resurrection of Jesus with the Jewish Passover is mentioned explicitly in the year 160 AD in Asia Minor by Melito of Sardis in an Easter homily. In that homily Melito of Sardis talks quite explicitly about the mystery of the Pasch and the mystery of the Lord.

The Paschal Mystery of Jesus Christ lies at the very centre of christian faith and discipleship. It is the story of redemption, the pattern of christian living, the creative source of new life, the paradoxical form of christian existence, and the peculiar shape of christian hope. There can be no authentic living of the gospel of Christ that is unfamiliar with the painful joy of the Paschal Mystery.

9   *S.C.*, a. 6 and a. 47.
10   *S.C.*, a. 81.

According to Vatican II, since Christ died for all, all human beings are touched, directly or indirectly, by the Paschal Mystery.[11] They are touched directly in so far as they become members of the christian community through baptism, and indirectly in so far as they follow 'the dictates of conscience' and/or 'strive to live a good life',[12] which demands a kind of anonymous dying and rising that finds its ultimate meaning in the Paschal Mystery of Christ. In virtue of the centrality of the Paschal Mystery for christian living, it is important to have some sense of the Paschal Mystery in the life of Jesus and in the life of the christian.

The Paschal Mystery in the Life of Jesus

The Paschal Mystery is a way of talking about the unity of the death and resurrection of Jesus or, better, the unity that belongs to the life, death, resurrection, ascension and Pentecost taken together as one single saving reality. The concept of the Paschal Mystery unifies the different aspects of the life of Jesus and guards against the fragmentation of the mystery of Christ. Some authors have focused almost exclusively on the public ministry of Jesus, others on the passion and death, and still others on the glorified risen Christ. A theology of the Paschal Mystery seeks to overcome this kind of imbalance. The words and deeds of Jesus are the context in which the death of Jesus takes place, and the death is the background against which the resurrection occurs. The preaching and teaching of Jesus give rise to the death and resurrection and the death and resurrection spell out the implications of the preaching and teaching. Without the cross, the resurrection would be just another statement about life after death similar to statements from other world religions. Likewise, without the resurrection, the cross could appear simply as a tragic ending of just another well-intentioned figure in history. To emphasise one aspect to the neglect of the other runs the risk of destroying the full range and richness of the mystery of Christ.

This underlying unity in the life of Jesus is brought out in a variety

11 *G.S.*, a. 22.
12 *L.G.*, a. 16.

of different images employed in the New Testament to describe the significance of the death and resurrection: movement, transition, passover, exodus, breakthrough. The life of Jesus is described in John's Gospel as a journey towards God the Father (Jn 16:5-18) or a departure out of this world to the Father (Jn 16:28), and by Luke as a transition from historical life in this world into eternal glory (Lk 24:26). The gospel stories convey a strong sense of historical movement in the life of Jesus which echoes the Jewish passover from slavery to freedom, a kind of exodus by Jesus from darkness to light, a going forth by Jesus in solidarity with humanity, a breakthrough by Jesus our brother to God our Father.

The goal of this journey by Jesus is the salvation of the world, symbolised in terms of the coming reign of God, the dawning of a new era, and the promise of eternal life. These realities are understood by the early Church to have been established through the death and resurrection of Jesus. The resurrection of Jesus from the dead is the dawning of a new era: 'the first fruits of those who have fallen asleep' (1 Co 15:20), 'the first born of all creation' (Col 1:15), the setting up of the 'new creation' (2 Co 5:17). Thus Paul can write with conviction:

> If Christ has not been raised from the dead, our preaching is in vain, our faith is futile, and we are still in our sins (1 Co 15:14).

The ultimate reason why Christ has been raised up is for our justification (Rm 4:25). Very early on in the life of the Church, as seen in chapter 3, the resurrection of Christ moved to the centre of the stage. Resurrection and salvation are very closely inter-connected. Acceptance of and adherence to the message of the resurrection is the basis of salvation (Rm 10:9). Even more important for the disciples of Christ was the challenge to become associated with the saving power of the death and resurrection of Christ. A new being, a new creation, a new spirit, has been introduced into our world through the death of Christ on the cross. The followers of Christ are invited to experience the liberating effects of this new paschal reality. Before exploring how this can happen, we need to grasp something of the historical unfolding of the Paschal Mystery in the life of Jesus.

When we look at the historical life and death of Jesus we discover that one of the most outstanding characteristics of this life is that it is a life lived out of love for others: the love of God the Father and the love of humanity. As noted in chapter 1, the life of Jesus is centred in the life-giving experience of God as Father and this experience carries with it a loving commitment to the freedom of others as sisters and brothers. When we probe this life of love, we discover that it is animated by the presence of a powerful paradox, the paradox of finding life through death and of losing one's life to save one's life. The spirit of this paradox is captured in the sayings of Jesus. Although these sayings have been worked over by the early Church in many instances, they do, none the less, sum up the underlying philosophy of the paradox animating the preaching and praxis of Jesus.

One example of such a paradox is the saying:

> Whoever would save his life will lose it, and whoever loses his life for my sake will save it (Mt 16:25).

This particular saying is repeated substantially another five times in the gospel accounts (Mk 8:35; Lk 9:24; Mt 10:39; Lk 17:33; Jn 12:25), a factor that points towards the authenticity of the saying. A stark contrast exists between saving one's life and losing one's life. The key to saving one's life is the ability to lose one's life. The historical context of this saying is the opposition to the ministry of Jesus. Jesus is becoming aware that he himself will be put to death by his opponents. Yet he intends to remain faithful to his mission of proclaiming the reign of God even if it means losing his life, because ultimately it will mean saving his life. It is in this context of the growing opposition to Jesus and his mission for the reign of God that this paradoxical advice is given to his disciples.[13]

A second example of the paradox operating in the preaching of Jesus can be found in the saying:

> Truly truly I say to you, unless a grain of wheat falls into the earth and dies, it remains alone; but if it dies it bears much fruit (Jn 12:24).

13 For a fuller analysis of this text see X. Léon-Dufour, *Life and Death in the New Testament: The Teaching of Jesus and Paul*, San Francisco: Harper and Row, 1986, pp. 32-35.

This saying points to the paradox that out of death comes life and that living fruitfully requires a kind of dying.

A third example, though exegetically quite complex, is the saying:

> If any one would come after me, let him deny himself and take up his cross and follow me (Mt 16:24; Mk 8:34; Lk 9:23).

Though this would seem to reflect the influence of the early Church because of the reference to the cross, there is a viewpoint which holds that the word 'cross' might refer here not to the historical cross of Jesus but to the injunction of Ezekiel to place a sign/mark/cross on the forehead to avoid being struck down by the angel of the Lord.[14] Whichever interpretation we give, the text itself calls for some form of self-denial for the sake of belonging to the other, in this case the person of Christ.

Other examples of the paradox of life through death and saving one's life by losing it can be found throughout the gospels. The call to conversion which involves a process of being reborn again (Jn 3:3-6) and the extensive reversal of values associated with the coming Reign of God capture other aspects of this paradox.

This striking paradox which permeates the preaching of Jesus comes to a particular climax in the historical death and resurrection. In and through this paschal event, it emerges that life does indeed come out of death. It is through the historical death of Jesus on the cross that the fullness of new life in resurrection comes. The strange paradox contained in the preaching of Jesus is confirmed and vindicated through the triumph of Jesus over death in resurrection. It now becomes clear that death after all does indeed give rise to new life and that the way to glory is the way of the cross. The philosophical paradox operative in the preaching of Jesus is illuminated by the historical paradox of the death and resurrection of Jesus. The paradoxical unity of life through death and of saving one's life by losing it is sharpened by the unity of the crucifixion and exaltation of Jesus. The co-existence of living and dying and of dying and living as found in the ministry of Jesus is radicalised in

---

14 Ezk 9:4-6. In favour of this interpretation see X. Léon-Dufour, op.cit., pp. 35-37.

the Paschal Mystery of Jesus at Calvary. This unity is most power-fully portrayed in John's Gospel where crucifixion and exaltation are presented as one event. The historical self-emptying love of Jesus comes to fruition on the cross as the fullness of life expressed in resurrection.

The Paschal Mystery of Christ represents a particular pattern of life, a special way of living, held out to the disciples of Christ: it embodies a new creative praxis for the followers of Christ. This new praxis has been described traditionally in terms of dying to the sinfulness that exists in the human heart. The dying involved is primarily a dying to the self in order to be reborn again, a type of self-renunciation, a form of self-denial with a view to rediscovering the self in relation to others.

For some commentators, especially feminists, this particular expression of the christian paradox appears too negative and self-deprecatory. Living in a culture, it is argued, that already inflicts inferiority upon women, there is already enough denial of the female self without demanding more. The female self seeks liberation from oppressive structures in society and not further self-denial. Likewise, those who are poor, hungry, or unemployed, are not interested in hearing about appeals to self-denial. There is already enough oppression of the self without looking for more.

Account must be taken of these difficulties when trying to express the heart of the christian message. The gospel of Christ, especially as expressed in the Paschal Mystery, is about good news: freedom and liberation, healing and wholeness, new life and communion. The paradox of christianity found at the centre of the Paschal Mystery of Christ is not something negative and oppressive; christianity is not a killjoy religion but a leaven of liberation bringing reconciliation and unity to that which is broken and estranged. The death and resurrection of Christ hold out a liberating promise to every human being. How then are we to express this liberating message of the Paschal Mystery of Christ, how can we communicate the paschal paradox that lies at the centre of the gospel, how do we translate the inner dynamism of the paradoxical sayings of Jesus?

In trying to find an answer to these questions, it must be pointed out that it is difficult to get away from the image of dying, not as an end in itself, not as a purely negative experience, but rather as the first step in a process that is empowering and liberating, an initial movement that frees the human spirit from its own debilitating self-imprisonment. Monica K. Hellwig talks about the need to de-centre the ego which exists in every human being. This involves a reluctant realisation 'that the centre and meaning of reality is not in one's self, but immediately in the human community and ultimately in God'.[15] Brendan Kennelly, expresses a similar truth when he writes that 'Self knows that self is not enough'.[16] James P. Mackey refers to the ego in each of us 'that has still not quite become a self'.[17] Each of these authors is really talking about one and the same paradox present in the sayings of Jesus and formalised for us in the Paschal Mystery. The paradox in question, at the heart of Christianity, is about the isolated ego becoming a relational being, the indifferent self becoming an active subject in solidarity with others, the lonely individual discovering his or her real centre of gravity in others and in God. The source inspiring this paschal movement/conversion is the living Spirit of the crucified and risen Christ. It is this peculiar pattern of dying to live, of passing over, of letting go, that is at the heart of the Paschal Mystery of Christ. Being a disciple of Christ involves the living out of this paradox.

The Paschal Mystery in the Life of the Christian

The christian enters the Paschal Mystery of Christ at three different levels in his or her life. These levels are the sacramental, the moral and the eschatological (the level of consummation). The sub-structure of each level is faith, love and hope respectively. At each stage the christian makes paschal contact with the crucified and risen Christ. Each contact with Christ involves a movement forward, a letting go of the ego and false idols, a personal process of dying and rising.

This dynamic of dying and rising can be discerned in its most

15 Monica K. Hellwig, *What Are They Saying about Death and Christian Hope?*, New York: Paulist Press, 1978, p. 15.
16 B. Kennelly, 'Connection', *The Voices*, Dublin: Gallery Books, 1973, p. 9.
17 J.P. Mackey, *Modern Theology*, Oxford: Oxford University Press, 1987, p. 187.

elementary form in relationships of friendship and love. Within these relationships people 'die' for the sake of the other. For example, spouses give themselves to each other in costly love and parents sacrifice themselves out of love for their children. This giving and dying can even involve physical death for the sake of the beloved which is the highest form of love there is. The life, teaching, praxis and death of Jesus exemplify this process of dying and rising. The life of Jesus, in particular the historical death and resurrection, is the pattern of christian discipleship and is lived out at the sacramental, moral and eschatological levels of historical existence.

On the sacramental level we make personal contact with the crucified and risen Christ in and through the different sacraments. This contact with Christ is initiated through the foundational sacrament of Baptism. According to the *Constitution on Sacred Liturgy* of Vatican II:

> By Baptism, men [women] are plunged into the Paschal Mystery of Christ: they die with him, are buried with him, and rise with him (cf. Rm 6:4; Ep 2:6; Col 3:1; 2 Tm 2:11).[18]

The word 'plunge' is well chosen here because it captures some of the dramatic effects associated with the liberating Spirit of the crucified and risen Christ. As a result of baptism, the self-centred ego is no longer an isolated ego but a self belonging organically to the Body of Christ. The christian now lives 'in Christ'. To use that rich Pauline expression means that she/he lives in a new relationship with the paschal Christ. Each one of the sacraments involves a paschal process of dying and rising, of passing over, and of letting go. In particular, the Eucharist is *the* celebration of the Paschal Mystery because the saving death and resurrection of Christ is recalled:

> For as often as you eat this bread and drink this cup you proclaim the Lord's death until he comes (1 Co 11:26).

In the Eucharist, the baptised members of the Body of Christ

18 *S.C.*, a. 6.

become one in Christ visibly and sacramentally and this unity in Christ is a foretaste of the future. The underlying supposition of each sacrament is faith and the basic characteristic of this faith is trust in the liberating Spirit released through the death and resurrection of Christ. The source of this faith is the gracious God who in the first instance created each and every human person for communion.

On the moral level we live out the Paschal Mystery in terms of our relationship with others. The ego moves out from being an ego to being a self in relationship with others. Venturing forth in relationship with others involves a dying and rising. A decentering of the ego requires a refocusing of the centre of gravity in one's life. This process is inspired by the great commandment of love. When we love, in the christian sense of *agape,* we die to something within us in order to relate more authentically to the other. To love is to break down the barriers that separate people from each other. The love of the christian which prompts this activity is the gracious love of God who first loved us. What happens on the moral level reflects what has already taken place on the sacramental level. What takes place morally is celebrated sacramentally. A mutually enriching relationship should obtain between the sacraments and morality.

On the eschatological level the Paschal Mystery touches human lives in terms of the future. Sooner or later the individual must face searching questions about the possibility of a lasting future. The relationship of the present to the future, and more specifically of the future to the present, is unavoidable. Indifference to one's own future and the future of others is difficult to sustain. The potential within every individual to become something more than he or she is carries within itself a promise for the future. This potential for growth as well as the peculiarly human capacity to anticipate is the first awakening of hope. Further, there is a basic openness within the human spirit towards a wholeness and completion that goes beyond all human possibilities. This openness directs the human spirit towards the possibility of fulfilment at some time in the future. Hope in a future of this kind requires a letting-go of self-centred interests, a trust in others and what the future has to offer. Such hope involves dying and rising, a self-surrendering into the promises of the future. The shape and form of that future have been given to us in outline in the death and resurrection of Christ, particularly in terms of the promise of resurrection. The object of christian hope is resurrection, not just of the individual but also of the community and the whole of creation.

These three different ways of living out the Paschal Mystery in the life of the christian are mutually complementary. Full appropriation of the death and resurrection of Christ requires the response of faith, hope and love. Within this threefold response there will always be a tension between what is and what is yet to come, between the present and the future, between being in Christ and becoming in Christ. This tension is caused by ego-centredness and the sinful social structures of the world in which we live. The passover from darkness to light, from sin to grace, from fragmentation to wholeness, is a fragile affair, allowing of more or less until the moment of death. Further, it must be emphasised that the Paschal Mystery of Christ affects not just individuals but also the members who make up the christian community and the whole of creation. A living, organic and affective unity exists between the individual, the community and creation. In virtue of this unity, St Paul can say that:

> If one member suffers, all suffer together; if one member is honoured, all rejoice together (1 Co 12:26).

Likewise, it is Paul who reminds us 'that the whole of creation has been groaning in travail' (Rm 8:22), awaiting the redemption of the Paschal Mystery of Christ. It cannot be emphasised enough, especially in these times of ecological crisis, that the redemption brought by the death and resurrection of Christ embraces the whole of creation. This unity between the individual, community and creation must be subjected to the liberating rhythms of the Paschal Mystery. Indeed, closer attention to the rhythms of nature, as we shall presently see, may help us to see more fully the new life that comes from living out the Paschal Mystery.

Immortality and/or Resurrection?

One of the purposes of a theology of the Paschal Mystery is to keep together the different aspects of the mystery of Christ and to ensure at the same time that all aspects of the Christ-Event have a direct bearing on christian living. The goal of the Paschal Mystery is the new life of resurrection. The paschal experiences of passing over from being an ego to being a self in relationships, and of losing one's life to save one's life, are oriented towards the gift of resurrection. Without the promise of resurrection, the experience of dying to self-centredness is at least ambiguous.

Yet, for most people living the christian life, the resurrection is hardly a dominant influence on their present-day living, whatever about the future. Indeed, for many, the reality of resurrection is understood as something that is rather remote and removed from the mainstream of christian living. The resurrection is perceived as something that took place back there in history two thousand years ago and that will take place some time in the distant future at the end of time with the second coming of Christ. In the meantime, however, the resurrection of Christ does not impinge in any real sense on the life of the christian. The doctrine of the resurrection of Christ and its implications are in fact quite marginal in the lives of many christians today. What is much more prominent in christian consciousness is the doctrine of the immortality of the soul. For many christians, life after death is about the immortality of the soul and not about the resurrection. The christian doctrine of the resurrection is understood as something that is at best reserved to the end of time. In response to the question, when does resurrection take place, most christians reply 'the resurrection occurs with the second coming of Christ'. Indeed, classical eschatology has an elaborate scheme which holds that at the moment of death the soul of the person, as immortal, enters into an 'intermediate state' of blessedness and from there awaits the resurrection of the dead at the end of time. Within this scheme of things there is very little room for the doctrine of the resurrection in terms of personal experience or in terms of what happens in death.

Here we find ourselves in the presence of two different traditions. On the one hand we have the theology of the Paschal Mystery, rediscovered at Vatican II, which emphasises the centrality of resurrection for christian living and the sacramental system. On the other hand we have the traditional theology which concentrates on the immortality of the soul and reserves resurrection to the end of time. Is it possible to reconcile these two particular emphases? Might it not be proposed that these two perspectives could complement each other and that the time is now ripe to go beyond both of these points of view to a new, higher synthesis?

A proper treatment of these questions cannot be undertaken here. The issues are too complex and the debates, in both the Middle Ages and in the contemporary period (mainly in Germany in the 1970s) are too vast to unravel.[19] The most that can be done here is to summarise some of the issues and to outline the direction of another possible point of view. This is perhaps best undertaken by looking at the strengths and weaknesses of the doctrine of the immortality of the soul *only,* and then going on to look at St Paul's theology of resurrection.

The doctrine of the immortality of the soul is deeply embedded in both the christian and religious consciousness of humanity. This important insight into the nature of the person owes its origin to Plato and has been the basis of our understanding of the dignity of the individual. It was adapted by christianity through its alliance with Hellenistic culture in the early centuries; it became part of christian doctrine in the Middle Ages and has been taught down through the centuries as an integral part of christianity. As a part of the christian tradition, it has stood the test of time. This doctrine holds that in every human person there is a spiritual centre and that

---

19 On the biblical and historical background see the following: K. Stendhal (ed.). *Immortality and Resurrection: Death in the Western World,* New York: 1969; P. Benoit and R. Murphy (eds.), *Immortality and Resurrection, Concilium,* No. 60, New York:, 1970; B. Marthaler, *The Creed,* Connecticut: Twenty-Third Publications, 1987, ch. 22. Instructive accounts of the debate in Germany are available in J. Ratzinger, *Eschatology: Death and Eternal Life,* Washington DC: The Catholic University Press of America, 1988, ch. V and Appendix I and II; W. Kasper, 'Hope in the Final Coming of Jesus Christ in Glory', *Communio: An International Catholic Review* 12 (Winter 1985), pp. 368-384; Z. Hayes, *Visions of a Future: A Study of Christian Eschatology,* Delaware: Michael Glazier, 1989, pp. 163-166.

this spiritual centre survives and subsists after death.[20] The immortality of the soul, therefore, is about the existence of a self-conscious element which survives the death of the physical body. Further, in emphasising the immortality of the soul and reserving the resurrection to the end of time, classical theology intended to bring out the incomplete character of salvation until all things are brought together in Christ at the second coming. In particular, classical theology affirms the individual immortality of the soul at death as distinct from the general resurrection of the dead at the end with a view to highlighting the social and organic dimensions of salvation. The destiny of the individual is somehow bound up with the destiny of the whole of humanity and therefore it cannot be finalised without reference to the destiny of the whole. The fullness of salvation for the individual, the community and creation will be realised only on the day of the general resurrection of the dead when Christ will be all in all. These strengths within the doctrine of the immortality of the soul must be measured against some of the contemporary difficulties that exist with an exclusive focus on this doctrine.

Foremost among these is the anthropological question of understanding what it might mean to talk about the survival of the spiritual core of a person in death. Is it possible to discuss the reality of a disembodied existence after death when the only form of existence that we know and experience is embodied? Further, given the classical understanding of the human person as an indissoluble unity of body and soul as well as the contemporary understanding coming from the hard sciences about the existence of a radical unity embracing all matter and spirit, it becomes increasingly difficult to talk about the existence of a purely spiritual element in the human person in isolation from some form of embodiment. In addition, references to the survival of the soul in death, awaiting the general resurrection of the dead, seem to have more in common with Jewish eschatology than christian eschatology as founded on the death and resurrection of Christ.

---

20 See 'Letter on Certain Questions in Eschatology', a.3, Congregation for the Catholic Faith, Rome, 1979.

St Paul on the Time of Resurrection

When we turn to the New Testament we find that the Pauline literature has much to say about the place of resurrection in christian living and dying. The letters of Paul and the literature influenced by Paul span a period of some fifteen years. The early Paul, believing that he would be alive for the second coming of Christ, emphasised links between resurrection and the Second Coming. For Paul the resurrection is directly connected with the second Coming of Christ:

> But we would not have you ignorant brethren, concerning those who are asleep... For this we declare to you by the word of the Lord, that we who are alive, who are left until the coming of the Lord, shall not precede those who have fallen asleep. For the Lord will descend from heaven ... and the dead in Christ will rise first; then we who are alive, who are left, shall be caught up together with them in the clouds to meet the Lord in the air. (1 Th 4:13-17; see also 1 Co 15:23-24).

With the passing of time Paul realises that he may not be alive for the second coming and so the emphasis shifts from the resurrection - parousia to an emphasis on death - resurrection. The later Paul, therefore, developed a theology for the interim period between the resurrection of Christ and the Second Coming. The focus now is on a mystical dying and rising with Christ in this life as a preparation for the next. Paul claims that resurrection for the individual begins in the present life and comes to some kind of fruition in death. He suggests that through baptism the christian is initiated into the resurrection of Christ:

> Do you not know that all of us who have been baptised into Christ Jesus were baptised into his death? We are buried therefore with him by baptism into death, so that as Christ was raised from the dead by the glory of the Father, we too might walk in newness of life ... so you must consider yourselves dead to sin and alive to God in Christ Jesus (Rm 6:3-4; see also Col 1:12).

The experience of 'being alive to God in Christ Jesus' for Paul is a constant struggle: 'Our outer nature is wasting away, our inner nature is being renewed every day' (2 Co 4:16) because we 'are being changed into his likeness from one degree of glory to another' (2 Co 3:18). This struggle is a process of dying and rising with Christ:

> For while we live we are always being given up to death for Jesus' sake, so that the life of Jesus may be manifested in our mortal flesh (2 Co 4:11).

For Paul this new and developing life 'in Christ' reaches a point of finality in death when individual resurrection takes place. In death our relationship with Christ comes to a point of fruition and a condition of individual resurrection is realised. The clearest expression of this is found in the Second Letter of Paul to the Corinthians:

> For we know that if the earthly tent we live in is destroyed, we have a building from God, a house not made with hands, eternal in the heavens. Here indeed we groan, and long to put on our heavenly dwelling, so that by putting it on we may not be found naked. For while we are still in this tent, we sigh with anxiety; not that we would be unclothed, but that we would be further clothed, so that what is mortal may be swallowed up by life (2 Co 5:1-5).

Most commentators suggest that in this text the earthly tent symbolises the physical body and the heavenly dwelling represents the new risen body given by God to the individual in death. A similar use of imagery can be found in the First Letter to the Corinthians:

> But someone will ask how are the dead raised? With what kind of body do they come? You foolish man. What you sow does not come to life unless it dies. And what you sow is not the body which is to be, but a bare kernel, perhaps of wheat or some other grain. God gives it a body as he has chosen, and to each kind of seed its own body (1 Co 15:35-38).

Here Paul is appealing to the analogy of the seed, also used by Jesus, to explain what happens in death. The seed falls into the ground and dies, and what comes up is a transformed stalk of wheat. For Paul something similar happens to the christian in death:

> What is sown is perishable
> What is raised is imperishable ...
> It is sown in weakness,
> It is raised in power.
> It is sown a physical body,
> It is raised a spiritual body (1 Co 15:43-44).

The image of the seed is a particularly powerful symbol of the resurrection that takes place in death. On the one hand it gets across the element of continuity and on the other hand it conveys the equally important element of transformation. Christian death and resurrection involve personal continuity within a process of transformation.

A further example in Paul that seems to suggest that individual resurrection takes place at death for the christian is the Letter to the Philippians 3. In part one of chapter 3, i.e. verses 2-11, Paul talks about the importance of knowing Christ in this life so that we may share his resurrection in the next:

> that I may know him and the power of his resurrection, and may share his suffering, becoming like him in his death, that if possible I may attain the resurrection from the dead (v. 10-11).

In part two of the same chapter, v. 12-21, Paul talks about the importance of keeping our eyes on the goal of resurrection in Christ in contrast to those who live as if there is no future except an earthly one:

> But our commonwealth is in heaven, and from it we await a saviour, the Lord Jesus Christ, who will change our lowly body to be like his glorious body (Ph 3:20-21).

A further theme in the writings of Paul suggesting that individual resurrection takes place in death is that of the gift of the Spirit. According to Paul the christian has been given the Spirit in baptism and it is this same Spirit that is the guarantee and the pledge of individual resurrection in the future:

> If the Spirit of him who raised Jesus from the dead dwells in you, he who raised Christ Jesus from the dead will give life to your mortal

body also through his Spirit who dwells in you (Rm 8:11; see also Rm 8:14-17; 2 Co 5:5).

These different texts in Paul suggest that the christian in history who has been dying and rising 'in Christ' will also be raised up in death with Christ into the new life of resurrection. What happens in death seems to go well beyond what might be called the immortality of the soul only. There is more than continuity implied; there is also change (1 Co 15:51-57; 2 Co 3:18), newness (2 Co 5:17), and transformation (1 Co 15:42-43). A real difference exists between the immortality of the soul which is about continuity and survival, and the resurrection of the body which is about the fulfilment and transformation of the individual. F.X. Durwell concludes his classical study on the resurrection with the following words:

> Pauline theology does not provide a single argument to show why the individual believer's resurrection should be delayed beyond death...Thus physical death completes sacramental death and all other deaths in a christian's life, all of which open out into the resurrection.[21]

But what, it will be asked, has become of the Second Coming of Christ in Paul? Has he given up altogether on the importance of the Second Coming? The short answer is no. There is an equally impressive body of texts in Paul which points towards the ultimate coming together of all things in Christ at the end of time. Paul has a vision of the future in which everything one day will be united in Christ. There is, according to Paul, 'a plan for the fullness of time, to unite all things in him (Christ), things in heaven and things on earth' (Ep 1:10). When this happens, then Christ will hand everything over to his heavenly Father: 'then comes the end, when he (Christ) delivers the kingdom to God the Father after destroying every rule and every authority and power' (1 Co 15:24-26), and 'when all things are subjected to him, then the Son himself will be subjected to Him who puts all things under Him that God may be everything to everyone' (1 Co 15:28).

---

21 F.X. Durwell, *The Resurrection: A Biblical Study*, London: Sheed and Ward, 1960, p. 347.

Reconciling Individual Resurrection and General Resurrection

How then are we to reconcile these two apparently different traditions in Paul? Must we collapse the biblical tradition about individual resurrection at the time of death into the tradition about the general resurrection at the end of time as classical theology seems to do, or must we conflate the tradition about the general resurrection of the dead at the end of time into 'resurrection at death' as some modern German theologians have done?[22] Is it perhaps possible to retain what is of value in these two traditions by introducing some important distinctions?

For example, might we not distinguish here between the individual resurrection that takes place in death and the general resurrection of the dead which occurs at the end of time? In other words, is it not possible to suggest that in death, individual resurrection takes place and that this individual resurrection will be completed and complemented at the end of time by the general resurrection of the dead? The Second Coming of Christ therefore will entail the gathering together of the whole people of God, the living on earth with those who have been raised up individually to new life in Christ, along with history and the fruits of history, and creation itself into 'a New Heaven and a New Earth' (Rv 21:1). In this vision, it should be clear that individual resurrection is incomplete without the general resurrection at the Second Coming, just as the part in isolation from the whole is incomplete. This incompleteness of individual resurrection is overcome through what might be called a process of socialisation and cosmic renewal that characterises the end of time. The christian who undergoes individual resurrection in death continues to retain a relationship with the pilgrim people of God on earth and indeed with creation itself. It is this relationship which is completed and transformed in the general resurrection of the dead at the end of time. In effect we are suggesting that resurrection is something that begins in this life through our paschal relationship with Christ, that this relationship

22 See the summary of the German debate in J. Ratzinger, *Eschatology*, op. cit. Appendices I and II.

with Christ comes to a point of fruition in death through individual resurrection, and that this personal resurrection is taken up into the general resurrection at the Second Coming.

What are the arguments in favour of this distinction between individual resurrection and general resurrection, and the particular vision it embodies? Does this vision have any advantages over the other points of view that we have looked at? Does it have any disadvantages and limitations?

The first point to note in favour of this vision is that it is more consistent with the language of christian living and liturgy. If through baptism and the Eucharist we are united to the crucified and risen Christ and therefore live 'in Christ', why should this relationship with Christ be severed in death through the immortality of the soul? Would it not be more consistent to suggest that our paschal relationship of dying and rising with Christ in this life comes to a point of fruition in the mystery of our death through individual resurrection?

Secondly, the proposal that resurrection begins in this life, reaches a climax in death, and is completed at the Second Coming gives a more unified vision of the full christian mystery. A relationship of both continuity and discontinuity is seen to exist between historical life in Christ, individual resurrection at death, and the general resurrection of the dead. The life of the christian develops in degrees between knowing Christ in this life, to personal resurrection in Christ at death, to being a part of the new creation of Christ at the end. The unity of belongingness with the crucified and risen Christ that marks christian existence obtains between the past, the present and the future. Further, this unified vision of life in Christ is more compatible with the emerging new story of the universe as a unified, relational and organic reality. Indeed it becomes possible within this new vision to talk about the cosmic dimensions of the Paschal Mystery in a way that is not immediately apparent with the immortality of the soul.[23]

Thirdly, the distinction between individual resurrection in death

23 Chapter 6 below outlines the New Story of the universe and indicates some of the correlations that might take place between it and the mystery of Christ.

and general resurrection at the end of time reflects more accurately the true nature of salvation as both individual and social. On the one hand the gift of salvation is about healing and making whole that which is wounded and fragmented. This sense of healing and wholeness is not immediately apparent in the doctrine of the immortality of the soul at death, whereas the possibility of individual resurrection in death does suggest at least the initiation of healing and wholeness, without prejudice to the reality of purgatory which may precede individual resurrection. Further, it is difficult to see how the immortality of the soul correlates adequately with the object of christian hope. The logic of christian hope is not the logic of inference which amounts to a desire for more of the same without limitations; it is this desire simply for continuity that corresponds to what is promised by the immortality of the soul. In contrast, the logic of christian hope is the logic of imagination which approximates more closely to what is promised in personal resurrection. On the other hand, by positing the general resurrection of the dead as something complementary in the future alongside individual resurrection, we are in fact safeguarding the all-important social character of salvation.

Fourthly, the suggestion that resurrection takes place in death and at the second coming of Christ is supportive of the emphasis given at Vatican II on the importance of the Paschal Mystery. We have already seen some of the implications of this emphasis: sacramental, moral and eschatological. Consistent with its own vision of the Paschal Mystery, Vatican II states, in at least two of its documents, that some individuals have already been raised up into glory. The *Constitution on the Sacred Liturgy* talks about the martyrs and the saints who have been 'Raised up to perfection by the manifold grace of God' and who are therefore 'already in possession of eternal salvation'. It then goes on to say:

> By celebrating the passage of these saints from earth to heaven the Church proclaims the Paschal Mystery as achieved in the saints who have suffered and been glorified with Christ.[24]

24 *S.C.*, a. 104.

Likewise, the *Dogmatic Constitution on the Church* affirms that certain individuals have already been raised up into glory without detracting from the Second Coming of Christ:

> When the Lord comes in his majesty ... death will be destroyed and all things will be subject to him ... Meanwhile some of his disciples are exiled on earth. Some have finished this life and are being purified. Others are in glory, beholding 'clearly God himself, triune and one, as he is'.[25]

The language and vision of these texts of Vatican II would seem to justify the distinction between individual resurrection and the general resurrection of the dead at the end of time.

A fifth and final point about this more unified vision is that it firmly places the resurrection at the centre of christian life and living. By restricting the doctrine of the resurrection to the end of time, classical theology unwittingly removed the centrality of resurrection from christian consciousness. This has created a void which has been filled by the immortality of the soul. The doctrine of the immortality of the soul, while expressing a permanently valid insight into the nature of the person, does not translate adequately the rich promises contained in the New Testament theologies of the death and resurrection of Christ. Further, the absence of a doctrine of the resurrection in contemporary christian consciousness is partly responsible for the current fascination among many christians with theories of reincarnation. A connection seems to exist between distorted views of the immortality of the soul and the possibility of a future reincarnation of the soul. In contrast, a christian theology which recognises the place of resurrection both in this life, in death and the second coming of Christ would seem to preclude the reincarnation of disembodied souls.

In putting forward this view of resurrection as something that begins in this life, that is realised in death for the individual, and is finalised at the general resurrection of the dead, we are not unaware of its limitations and the outstanding questions it leaves unanswered. For example, it is quite difficult to describe what is involved in individual resurrection in death. Clearly we are talking

25 *L.G.*, a. 49, cf. also a. 51.

about some form of personal fulfilment and transformation of individual embodied existence. How can this take place, how do we describe this, given the rupture of relationships that takes place at death and the fact that the physical body goes into the earth and perishes? Closely connected to this question is the equally problematic task of giving a credible account of what is symbolised by the second coming of Christ.

A second cluster of questions concerns the complicated issue of the relationship that exists between time and eternity, between history and the next world. The only way we can talk about eternity is through the image of temporal sequences.

A third area requiring further attention is the meaning of theological language in the context of death and eternity. Theological language has in this area many very obvious limitations. For instance, when we talk about 'life after death', we are using the concept of 'life' in a sense quite different from the meaning of this word in the context of 'life before death'. Eschatological language is highly symbolical and analogical, heavily dependent on the non-literal import of images.

The existence of such outstanding questions is an important and necessary antidote against 'arbitrary imaginative representations: excess of this kind is a major cause of the difficulties Christian faith often encounters'[26] in dealing with the situation of humanity after death.

Images of Resurrection

By way of conclusion to this pastoral theology of the Paschal Mystery and in support of our suggestion that resurrection affects life before death as well as life after death, we will close with a short account of some images that might convey the rich meaning of resurrection. It should be abundantly clear at this stage that there is a basic unity between death and resurrection. There is no resurrection without death, and the death of the individual without resurrection would be the final absurdity of life. We all wish to bask

26 'Letter on Certain Questions in Eschatology' a.7, Congregation for the Catholic Faith, Rome, 1979. See also *L.G.*, a. 51.

in the glory of resurrection but we shirk the way to resurrection which is the way of the cross. There is no glory without the cross, and so the law of life for the christian becomes the law of the cross/*lex crucis*.

There are certain traces or intimations of this law of the cross as the key to resurrection all around us in life: the seasons of the year, the rhythm of nature, the cycle of life and the evolutionary processes, each in their own way disclose a paschal pattern of life through death. Some of these intimations in nature have been more keenly observed by poets than by theologians. It was Shelley who said:

> If winter comes,
> Can spring be far behind?

Or again, Francis Thompson reminds us:

> It is the falling acorn that buds the tree,
> The falling rain that bears the greenery,
> Fern plants moulder when the ferns arise,
> For there is nothing lives but something dies.
> And there is nothing dies but something lives.

When we look at the cycle of life we notice that the living cell must divide in order to reproduce. The classic example here, the one used by Jesus and St Paul, is that of the seed which must die in order to bring forth fruit (Jn 12:24; 1 Co 15:36-38). The acorn dies to produce the oak tree and the caterpillar changes to give rise to the butterfly. These are examples of resurrection in slow motion and as such they capture the important elements of identity within transformation which we associate with the resurrection of the individual. Christians, like the acorn and the caterpillar, are called to be butterflies and oak trees!

At the human level of life itself we know that birth is a death to life in the womb and that this birth is the first of a series of deaths through which we begin to live more fully. The image of being reborn is used by Jesus to get across the dying and rising required for entry into the coming Reign of God. The experience of growing up from childhood to puberty to adolescence to adulthood to some kind of maturity is a process of dying to rise to fuller forms of life. As Goethe once remarked:

> If you have not understood
> the command: 'die and become',
> You are but an obscure transient,
> on a shadow of an earth.

In a similar way psychological development often requires that we die to certain fears and phobias that impede life within us so that we may grow and expand our being in existence. The trouble is, as S. Parker, the playwright points out:

> We are a tribe who has lost the knowledge of how to die.[27]

These particular examples symbolise the continuous process of dying and rising in life which prepares the individual for resurrection in death.

Another powerful symbol of what is involved in resurrection may be taken from the evolutionary processes that have taken place in the world around us. Evolutionary jumps from inorganic to organic life, from plant life to human life, have been accompanied by intense moments of constriction which in turn have given birth to new forms of life. The evolutionary leap forward symbolises the final breakthrough and novelty that awaits the individual in resurrection at death through the grace of Christ and the creative activity of the Spirit of God in the world.

Finally, an image of resurrection may be taken from the experience of sowing and harvesting, used so often in the parables of growth concerning the coming Reign of God (Mk 4:3ff; Mt 13:31ff). Resurrection is about the gathering up into full flower all the seeds of justice, peace and love that have been sown in this life into the new creation at the end of time. We know from the gospel that there is no christian justice, peace and love without conversion and a personal process of dying and rising. The final harvesting in death is related in some way to the sowing in this life, even though 'no eye has seen nor ear heard, nor heart of man conceived, what

---

27 S. Parker, *Night Shades.*

God has prepared for those who love him' (1 Co 2:9). Care must always be taken not to confuse images of resurrection with the full reality of resurrection which lies beyond all categories of space and time. In truth, as we have already seen in our last chapter, the best understanding of resurrection is given to us by saying what it is not, because in saying what it is not we are beginning to glimpse darkly what it is.

Ultimately the question of resurrection is a question about death. We will never know what the mystery of the resurrection is about unless we first of all know and experience death. The death involved in resurrection is not simply a physical death at the end of life; it is a death that must begin to take place now in terms of a daily dying and passing over. It is only when we know how to decentre the ego from its self-enclosed world that we can begin to glimpse the promise of resurrection. This means, in effect, that as we go through life we must summon up the courage to risk dying daily in order to find ourselves, to let go of the ego to find the self in its human and divine relationship. If we fail to do this during life, it is unlikely that we will know how to surrender ourselves at death into the gracious presence of the triune God. The real preparation for death is learning how to live more fully now by dying daily and letting go of slavish idols. The purpose of a theology of the Paschal Mystery is to bring about that learning process in this life, so that we may be ready to die with faith, love and hope in our hearts at death. When this happens we will be more at ease with the words of Tennyson:

> Behold we know not anything,
> I can but trust that good shall fall,
> At last, far off, at last to all,
> And every winter change to spring *(In Memoriam)*.

6

The Doctrine of the Incarnation: Human and Cosmic Considerations

The doctrine of the Incarnation stands at the centre of christian faith and is the bedrock for our understanding of the major truths of christianity: the Trinity, the Church, the sacraments, grace, and eschatology. In broad terms the Incarnation is the doctrine about Jesus of Nazareth as the Son of God made human. Biblically speaking, it is summed up in the statement that the eternal word of God was made flesh and dwelt among us (Jn 1:14). This is usually expressed in the story of God coming down from heaven and entering fully into the human condition in the life and death of Jesus. The Incarnation has tended to be associated with the infancy narratives of the New Testament and is understood to have been inaugurated at the time of the annunciation.

Theologically speaking the biblical account of the Incarnation is usually expressed in the technical language of the two nature-one person model formulated at the Council of Chalcedon (451). Jesus possesses a fully human nature and a fully divine nature which exist in one single person who is the Logos of God. Jesus is presented as true God and true man; he is the eternal Son of God made flesh; he is the personal presence of God in the world.

The classical presentation of these basic truths of the Incarnation has been shaped by the Councils of Nicea (325), Ephesus (431) and especially Chalcedon (451). The Council of Chalcedon provided the philosophical framework which has successfully held together the christological dogma of the Incarnation for the last sixteen hundred years. The Chalcedonian framework is hallmarked by the complex philosophical categories of substance, nature and person.

In recent times, however, the classical presentation of Chalcedon has come in for serious criticism. It is pointed out that the technical language of substance, nature and person no longer communicates today what it did at the time of the great christological councils. Further, it is complained that these technical terms have been understood in an overly static and essentialist manner. Most of all, it is argued that the Chalcedonian framework bears little or no visible relationship to the historical life, death and resurrection of Jesus as understood by modern exegesis. It should be noted that these observations are directed not against the truth of the Incarnation as expressed at the Council of Chalcedon but rather at the language and the non-historical terms of that Council's declaration.

Vatican II, conscious of the changes that have taken place in this century, pointed out:

> The human race has passed from a static concept of reality to a more dynamic, evolutionary one. In consequence there has arisen a new series of problems, a series as important as can be, calling for new efforts of analysis and synthesis.[1]

The doctrine of the Incarnation is one of those areas in theology which at present calls for a new synthesis as a result of the shift from a static view of reality to a more dynamic, evolutionary position. The classical understanding of the Incarnation has been cast in a closed, static and unhistorical framework. Given the emergence of historical consciousness and philosophical pluralism today, it has become increasingly difficult to communicate the truth of the Incarnation in the technical language of Chalcedon without being misunderstood. Consequently, it has become necessary to move beyond the classical framework and language in a manner that seeks at the same time to safeguard the underlying doctrinal

---

1   *G.S.*, a. 5; see also a. 4, 36, and 62.

truth of Chalcedon. In setting out to do this we should remember the principle enunciated by Pope John XXIII and adopted by Vatican II:

> For the deposit of faith or revealed truths are one thing; the manner in which they are formulated without violence to their meaning and significance is another.[2]

Faithful to its own principles, Vatican II does in fact talk about the Incarnation in a language and framework that goes beyond Chalcedon. The Council points out that:

> The faith is that only in the mystery of the Incarnate Word does the mystery of man take on light ... Christ, the final Adam, by the revelation of the mystery of the Father and his love, fully reveals man to man himself and makes his supreme calling clear... For by his incarnation the Son of God has united himself in some fashion with every man. He worked with human hands, he thought with a human mind, acted by human choice, and loved with a human heart.[3]

Clearly the focus here is on the human, anthropological significance of the Incarnation. The mystery of the Incarnation reveals the Son of God to the world, but it also reveals the dignity and destiny of every human being. Jesus Christ as the Word Incarnate is the key to a proper understanding of what it means to be fully human. Clearly the anthropological aspects of the Incarnation are to the fore here at Vatican II.

A more recent statement of the doctrine of the Incarnation by Pope John Paul II takes up the emphasis of Vatican II and adds significantly to it:

> The Incarnation of God the Son signifies the taking up into unity with God not only human nature, but in this human nature, in a sense, of everything that is flesh ... The Incarnation then, also has a cosmic significance, a cosmic dimension: the 'first born of creation' unites himself in some way with the entire reality of man, within the whole of creation.[4]

2   *G.S.*, a. 62.
3   *G.S.*, a. 22.
4   *Dominum et Vivificatum (On the Holy Spirit in the life of the Church and the World)*, Vatican City: 1986, a. 50.

According to this statement there are two fundamental truths contained in the mystery of the Incarnation. Firstly, the Incarnation is about God taking up human nature into the self of God. Secondly, the Incarnation also embraces the whole of creation as part of the new and special relationship that now obtains between God and humanity; this latter point is referred to as the cosmic aspect of the Incarnation.

There are, therefore, at least two aspects to the mystery of the Incarnation that are worth exploring. These are the anthropological and the cosmological. The anthropological concerns the ontological relationship that exists between God and humanity exemplified in the historical life, death and resurrection of Jesus as the Word made flesh; this relationship between God and humanity has special significance for the way we understand the human condition. The cosmological aspect concerns the relationship between God and the cosmos disclosed in the mystery of Jesus Christ. It is surely important today to keep together both the anthropological and the cosmological aspects of the Incarnation, given the damaging ecological consequences of separating the human from the cosmic in recent times. The purpose of this chapter will seek to explore the anthropological and cosmological significance of the Incarnation.

The Image of God and the Human Person in Classical Christology

In going beyond Chalcedon it is, of course, necessary to be aware of some of the difficulties inherent in the classical presentation of christology. These difficulties circle around the image of God and the image of the human person associated with the Chalcedonian dogma.

The image of God coming down from heaven to earth at the time of the Incarnation seems to imply unwittingly the introduction of a previously absent divine presence into the world. Little or no account is taken of the general presence of God in the created world and among the people of God in the history of Israel. If anything, the Incarnation seems to take place in separation from God's all-pervasive presence in the world. As a result the

Incarnation comes across as a 'bolt out of the blue', giving the impression that it is more of an isolated exception than a definitive disclosure of God's presence in the world.[5] The Incarnation therefore is in danger of coming across as something of an interruption of the normal processes of God's presence in the world, appearing as a temporary divine intrusion which is terminated with the ascension of Christ. The imagery of God coming down and going up is contrary to the real meaning of the Incarnation which can be summed up in the language of Emmanuel, that is, God permanently with us.

A similar problem arises when we look at the understanding of the human person involved in the classical account of the Incarnation. When we say God became flesh in Jesus, the impression is often given that God takes over the human person Jesus and that the humanity of Jesus from the moment of his birth onwards is somehow divinely pre-determined. The freedom of the man Jesus seems to be eliminated and this in turn negates the existence of human responsibility, merit or value attaching to anything Jesus does throughout his mission and ministry. The man Jesus appears to be a purely passive recipient in the mystery of the Incarnation.

The source of these impressions is the static and non-historical framework in which the divine-human drama of the Incarnation is expressed by the Council of Chalcedon. If we are to do justice to the historical interplay that takes place between God and humanity in Jesus, then more attention will have to be given to the freedom of the man Jesus. In fact one of the most effective criteria for safeguarding the historical character of the Incarnation is that of paying particular attention to the freedom of Jesus.[6]

A further difficulty in the classical framework of the Incarnation is the suggestion that the identity and vocation of Jesus are somehow fixed and determined at birth. Yet we know in the light of modern

5   J.A.T. Robinson, 'Need Jesus have been Perfect?', *Christ, Faith and History*, S.W. Sykes and J.P. Clayton (eds.), London: Cambridge University Press, 1972, p. 39.
6   See D. Gray, 'The Divine and Human in Jesus', *Proceedings of the Catholic Theological Society of America*, vol. 31 (1976), pp. 21-39.

psychology that self-identity is not something determined solely at birth. The human person is not born into the world with a fixed identity. On the contrary, authentic self-identity is that which emerges historically out of a complex series of experiences and relationships in freedom with others in the world. In reality, the emergence of human self-identity is something that becomes fixed and final at death and not at birth. Self-identity, therefore, is a developing historical reality which is permanently in a process of becoming. This does not mean that the development of self-identity is an independent, free-floating affair in the life of the individual. Rather, personal identity is shaped by the environment of one's life from birth onwards; it results from the interplay between individual freedom and human destiny. The self is constituted through a series of personal experiences and free relationships with the world and other selves. The self-in-becoming is an historical outcome rather than a predetermined given at birth.

The Need for a New Perspective

It should be clear from these brief observations on the images of God and the human person implicit in the traditional framework of the Incarnation that there is a need for a change in perspective. This change is best summed up in what Bernard Lonergan called the shift from a classical culture to the rise of historical consciousness.[7] Broadly speaking there has been a move, especially in this century, away from the perception of cultural forms as fixed and closed to an understanding of culture that is thoroughly historical and open-ended. The world as we experience it is no longer understood as something determined and immutable; instead it is experienced as an unfinished project which is still under construction. In particular, this shift in consciousness has affected our understanding of the place of the individual in the world. The human person is no longer studied as an 'object' out there in a given position but as a 'subject'

7   B. Lonergan, 'Theology in its New Context', *The Theology of Renewal,* vol. 1, L.K. Shook (ed.), New York: Herder and Herder, 1968, pp. 34-46; 'The Transition from a Classicist Worldview to a Historical-Mindedness', *A Second Collection,* W. Ryan and B. Tyrell (eds.), London: Darton, Longman and Todd, 1974, pp. 1-9.

who is personally responsible for the shaping of his or her destiny. We look at the individual from 'the inside out' and not from 'the outside in'.[8] The human person is a subject, a radically relational subject, who develops historically through relationships with other subjects.

Further, not only the human person but also the world around the person is understood to be radically relational, processive, and interdependent. The world in which we live is a vast network of web-like relationships, dynamic processes and organic inter-connections. A fundamental unity is perceived to exist between spirit and matter, self and world, subject and object – a unity that has been significantly enlarged and enriched by the findings of post-modern cosmologies which we will take up more explicitly when dealing with the cosmic dimensions of the Incarnation.

Before applying this changed historical and relational perspective to the mystery of the Incarnation we need to say something, by way of introduction, about the overall relationship that exists between God and the world. In some respects the question about the meaning of the Incarnation today is as much a question about the general presence of God in the world as it is a question about the particular presence of God in Jesus of Nazareth. The Incarnation of God in Jesus took place in a particular historical and religious context. Some understanding of this context is necessary if we are to make sense out of the christian claim that God was personally present in Jesus of Nazareth. Without some reference to this context, the Incarnation may well appear as an anomalous exception to the general presence of God in the world before and after the Christ-event.

Situated in this larger context, the Incarnation will begin to be seen as the personalisation and crystalisation of God's overall presence in the world. How then are we to understand God's general relationship to the world and history as context for the particular Incarnation of God in Jesus?

The God of the Hebrew scriptures is a God who exists in sharp contrast to the immutable, detached, unmoved mover of Greek

8   B. Lonergan, 'The Subject', *A Second Collection*, London: Darton, Longman and Todd, 1974, pp. 69-86.

philosophy. The God of the people of Israel is a personally active, dynamic and involved God made known to the Israelites through their experience of history:

> The Lord said 'I have seen the affliction of my people who are in Egypt, and have heard their cry because of their taskmaster; I know their sufferings, and I have come to deliver them out of the land of the Egyptians, and to bring them out of that land ... and now behold the cry of the people has come to me, and I have seen the oppression with which the Egyptians oppress them. Come I will send you to Pharaoh ...'(Ex 3:7-10).

The unfolding of Hebrew history is the unfolding of a God who journeys faithfully with the people of Israel.[9] The God of Israelite experience is equally the God of the liberating exodus and painful exile. This strong sense of God's constant presence is formulated in Israel's faith in God as creator portrayed in the creation narratives of the Book of Genesis, in many psalms, and in the Wisdom literature. God who is active in history is the same God who in the beginning created the heavens and the earth (Gn 1:1), who fills the whole world and ... holds all things together (Ws 1:7). It is the same personal God of Jewish history and creation from the beginning who is the subject of the Incarnation.

Before taking up the doctrine of the Incarnation, reference must be made to the story of humanity's faith response to God's presence in history and creation as a backdrop to the Christ-event. Here we should remember that the personal act of faith is always a free act. The presence of God in the world does not coerce the individual into belief. To the contrary, the divine presence in history and creation is experienced as a gracious invitation and a persuasive calling to the free act of personal trust and self-surrender. The individual lives out his or her life within the ambit of a disarming, gracious presence.

In broad terms every human person experiences himself or herself as a self-transcending being, a being who reaches out beyond the self towards some unifying centre of communion, a being who

---

9   This theme is most helpfully developed by D. Carroll in A *Pilgrim God for a Pilgrim People*, Dublin: Gill and Macmillan, 1988, especially in ch. 3.

experiences an unrestricted desire to know and to love, a being who is restless in virtue of his or her awareness of human incompleteness. The goal of this searching self-transcendence is the elusive mystery we call God. At the same time the individual discovers within this experience that he or she is nonetheless estranged from this goal of self-transcendence. The human self experiences at the same time a real sense of both belongingness to and separation from the holy mystery we call God. It is this common human experience of God that lies behind the colourful story of Israel's faith in Yahweh. It is, in particular, this story of God's gracious self-communication to the individual and the community in history and creation and at the same time the individual's and community's incomplete response to this invitation that sets the stage for the historical process of the Incarnation.

The Historical Drama of the Incarnation

We have seen, in broad strokes, that God communicates God's self through creation and history and that the individual person, through the experience of a searching self-transcendence, responds in faith to this divine presence. It is in the light of this structure of God's gracious self-giving and the individual's fragile response in faith that we can now turn explicitly to the divine-human and human-divine exchange that took place historically in Jesus of Nazareth. The story of God's gracious self-communication in history and humanity's restless self-transcendence come to a unique point of contact in the historical life, death and resurrection of Jesus. God and the human person come together in perfect unity in Jesus; the divinity of Jesus is co-present/active in and through the sacred humanity of Jesus. A real unity, a hypostatic unity as the Council of Ephesus called it, is established between the divine and the human, between infinite self-giving and human receiving in freedom, between heaven and earth, once and for all in the life of Jesus.

When we look at the life of Jesus we discover that the activity of God's gracious self-communication is at work in a particular and even more intense manner. God's personal outreach to human nature in the person of Jesus is deeper than heretofore in the history of Israel. The divine self-giving to humanity is on the one hand continuous with the previous activity of God in creation and history. On the other hand, it is important to stress that there is a qualitative difference in the divine outreach given in Jesus. This difference in the quality of the divine self-giving is expressed and symbolised in the biblical narratives surrounding the birth, the baptism, the transfiguration and the death of Jesus.

This new divine initiative is personally addressed to the man Jesus throughout his life. As in the case of every divine invitation, the one addressed is free to accept or to reject the call. Examples of the challenging character of the divine call can be seen in the temptations of Jesus in the desert, in the garden of Gethsemane, and on the cross. On the other hand, moments like the baptism at the Jordan, the reading of the prophet Isaiah in the synagogue at Nazareth, the journey up to Jerusalem, the cleansing of the temple, are indications of Jesus' consistent openness, receptivity and faithfulness to the divine call. Clearly the horizon of the life of Jesus is shaped and influenced from beginning to end by his unique awareness of this divine call and his continuous experience of the co-presence of God in his life. In particular, as we have seen in chapter 1, it was Jesus' experience of God as *Abba* that informed his mission and ministry. The experience of God as Father is the basis of his self-understanding as the Son of God and the source of his understanding of the coming Reign of God. It is these historical realities in the ministry of Jesus, namely the experience of God as Father, the strong sense of a filial relationship with the Father, the unfolding awareness of the nearness of the Reign of God, the consciousness of being sent by God to represent God and to do the work of God that provide the key to the divine identity of Jesus.

As noted earlier, self-identity is something that unfolds historically in and through different experiences and relationships in life. We do not come into the world with a pre-determined identity. Rather we leave the world at death with a historically achieved self-identity. To be sure, the circumstances of our entry into the world play an important role in the achievement of identity, as they most surely did in the case of Jesus. At the same time the circumstances of entry into life have to be worked out historically through the exercise of personal freedom. A delicate relationship exists between the interplay of destiny and freedom, identity and history in the life of Jesus.

In the case of Jesus, we can say that the identity of Jesus is influenced historically by the quality and character of his free response to God's unique call. The whole life of Jesus is God-shaped and kingdom-centred, so much so that the subjectivity of Jesus is intimately connected with the subjectivity of God the Father which is permanently present to Jesus. It is in and through the multiplicity of these continuous experiences and relationships that the true identity of Jesus as the eternal Word of God incarnate emerges.

The interaction that takes place between God's gracious outreach and the obedient response in faith to this divine outreach is such that Jesus is historically revealed as the Word made flesh, the eternal Son of God incarnate. The personal identity of Jesus, therefore, may be said to be co-constituted by the activity of God reaching deep down into the heart of human nature and that human nature freely accepting the divine summons in the life of Jesus. The Christ-event is that which is effected historically from the perfect union between God and the human in Jesus. As a result of this unity between God and humanity, Jesus is personally God in human form, the eternal Word of God made flesh.

An example of what is involved in the historical constitution of Jesus' divine identity may be taken from the domain of interpersonal relationships. The reciprocal love that exists between a husband and a wife is such that historically over a period of time the husband may incorporate into his own self-identity certain aspects and dimensions of the beloved's personality and vice versa. The encounter between the two subjectivities shapes the development of a new self-identity in the husband or the wife as the case may be. A similar process can occur in the experiences and the relationships that take place between a father and his son or a mother and her daughter. The son realises his own self-identity through a series of different experiences in life. A formative factor within these identity-shaping experiences will be the experience he has of his own father and the particular regard the son has for the father. If there is a close bond between the father and the son, then there is a sense in which the son will incorporate the characteristics of his father into his own personality.

In an analogous manner we can say that Jesus, through a process of permanent openness to the Spirit of God the Father, is the perfect expression of the Father as Son. This process of divine-human and human-divine activity is instituted before the birth of Jesus. From his conception onwards Jesus is uniquely destined to be the Son of God Incarnate. The divine destiny of Jesus, however, has to be worked out historically in and through the free exercise of trust and love. While it is necessary to emphasise the particular initiative of God in the Incarnation from the conception of Jesus onwards, it is equally important to focus on the freedom of the man Jesus in responding to this divine initiative. To this extent we must say that the Incarnation was a historical process instituted by God at the conception of Jesus, which was subsequently sustained and perfected by the loving response in freedom of Jesus. A balance must be maintained between the divine risk of predestining the man Jesus to be the Son of God incarnate and the human freedom of Jesus in successfully living out that divine destiny.

It is this historical perspective that the so-called New Testament adoptionist texts were trying to communicate. In his introduction to the Letter to the Romans, Paul points out that God 'designated Jesus Son of God in power according to the spirit of holiness by his resurrection from the dead' (Rm 1:3-4).[10] The author of the Letter to the Hebrews reminds us that Jesus 'learnt obedience through what he suffered and being made perfect, he became the source of eternal salvation' (Heb 5:8-9). Further, St Luke tells his audience that the Jesus whom they crucified, 'God has made him both Lord and Christ' (Ac 2:36). In each instance there is a strong sense of the historical and processive character of the Incarnation.

Traces of this understanding of the mystery of the Incarnation can

---

10 A legitimate alternative translation for 'designated', according to the RSV, is 'constituted'.

be found among contemporary christologists. Two examples will suffice here. Walter Kasper, in his book *Jesus the Christ*, notes how the indeterminate and open aspect that belongs to the human person is determined definitively by the unity of the person with the Logos. As a result of this unity of Jesus' human person with the eternal Logos, human personality comes to its absolute unique fulfilment.[11] In other words the encounter between the personality of Jesus and the eternal Logos effects the fulfilment of human personality. This encounter does not diminish the human personality but rather brings it to completion and perfection.

A second example worth mentioning here is that of John Cobb who wrote an article entitled 'A Whiteheadian Christology' in 1971 and later developed this into a book entitled *Christ in a Pluralistic Age*.[12] According to Cobb the presence of the Logos in the world constitutes the selfhood of Jesus. During his life Jesus chose freely to constitute his selfhood as one with the presence of God and by doing this he was the fullest Incarnation of the Logos in the universe. This view likewise resembles in broad outline the basic perspective being proposed here for a historical and processive understanding of the Incarnation. In noting this broad agreement with Cobb's christology we would want however to question his apparent neglect to bring out clearly enough the special and qualitatively new initiative taken by God in instituting this process in Jesus.

In Search of the Cosmic Dimension of the Incarnation

Having explored some of the aspects involved in 'the taking up into unity with God ... of human nature' we can now attempt to seek

11 W. Kasper, *Jesus the Christ,* London: Burns & Oates, 1976, p. 248. Echoes of the same kind of thinking can be found in K. Rahner, 'Current Problems in Christology', *Theological Investigations,* vol. 1, London: DLT, 1961, pp. 183-184; E. Schillebeeckx, *Jesus: An Experiment in Christology,* London: Collins, 1979, p. 656. A helpful and more elaborate account of the complex issues involved here can be found in A. Baxter, 'Chalcedon and the Subject in Christ', *The Downside Review,* January 1989, pp. 1-21.
12 J. Cobb, 'A Whiteheadian Christology', *Process Philosophy in Christian Thought,* D. Browne, R.E. James, and G. Reeves (eds.), Indianapolis: Bobbs-Merrill Company, Inc., 1971, pp. 382-398; *Christ in a Pluralist Age,* Philadelphia: Westminster Press, 1975.

out 'the cosmic dimension of the Incarnation'. In trying to talk about the cosmic dimension of the Incarnation we are really asking questions about the relationship of Christ to the whole of the universe: does the mystery of Christ have anything to say to our present understanding of the world in which we live? does the significance of the Incarnation extend beyond the salvation of human beings and their history?

Discussions about the cosmic Christ have not been to the fore in the christological renaissance of the last thirty years, nor indeed in the christology of the last two to three hundred years.[13] Jaroslav Pelikan is surely right when he says the main reason for this neglect is that the 'enlightenment philosophy deposed the cosmic Christ'.[14] The philosophy of Enlightenment, inspired by the discovery of the scientific method in the seventeenth century gave rise to cosmologies that were inimical to christology. The separation of faith and reason had the effect of putting christology on the sideline of the dialogue with developments in science. Further, the situation was compounded by the existence of changing cosmologies. For example, the shift from a geocentric universe to the heliocentric universe of Copernicus and the move from Newtonian mechanism to Einstein's theory of relativity and quantum physics did not encourage contact between christology and cosmology. In addition, the persistent presence during this period of a dualism between nature and grace pre-empted any kind of critical correlation between the theology of Incarnation and a 'scientific' understanding of the world. As a result there is little or no theology of the cosmic Christ in modern christology, even though there is the presence of a cosmic christology in the Synoptics, St Paul, St John and the Greek Fathers as we shall see presently.

In contrast to this lacuna in christology, there is at present a new quest of the cosmic Christ in train which is comparable to the quest

13 There are some notable exceptions to this statement. The most outstanding is Teilhard de Chardin who had much to say about the cosmic Christ in his diaries and published works. See J. Lyons, *The Cosmic Christ in Origen and Teilhard de Chardin: A Comparative Study,* Oxford: Oxford University Press, 1982.
14 J. Pelikan, *Jesus Through the Centuries: His Place in the History of Culture,* Newhaven and London:Yale University Press, 1985, p. 182.

of the historical Jesus that took place in the 1950s and 1960s.[15] This quest of the cosmic Christ has been brought to the fore by the emergence of a new cosmic consciousness concerning the immensity and antiquity of the universe we live in. This in turn has resulted in a series of significant developments in the last decade or so which raise questions either explicitly or implicitly about the relationship of Christ to the cosmos. These developments include the emergence of creation-centred theologies,[16] the promotion of a new dialogue between science and religion,[17] the rediscovery of the importance of cosmology,[18] and the recognition of an ecological crisis.[19] What is the relationship of the Incarnation to creation? Can christian faith engage in a meaningful dialogue with the new stirrings in science? Is the care of the earth a purely practical expedient or a christian responsibility rooted in the Incarnation?

These theological shifts have resulted in a new appreciation of the importance of cosmology. Cosmological assumptions concerning origins of the universe and the structure of the world as a whole do have a bearing on the way we understand theology and, in particular, on how we see the place of Christ in relation to creation. Indeed the credibility of christology in the future will depend to a large degree on its ability to enter into a meaningful conversation with the emerging post-modern cosmologies. Of course, part of the

---

15 The emerging literature on cosmic christology would include the works of T. de Chardin; J.A. Lyons, *The Cosmic Christ in Origen and Teilhard de Chardin: A Comparative Study,* Oxford: Oxford University Press, 1982; J. Pelikan, 'The Cosmic Christ', *Jesus Through the Centuries*, pp. 57-70.; G. Strachan, *Christ and the Cosmos*, Dunbar, 1985; I. Bergeron and A. Ernst, *Le Christ universel et l'évolution selon T. de Chardin*, Paris, 1986.

16 See D. Carroll, *Towards a Story of the Earth*, Dublin: Dominican Publications, 1988; G. Daly, *Creation and Redemption*, Dublin: Gill and Macmillan, 1988.

17 H. Rolston, *Science and Religion: A Critical Survey*, Philadelphia: Temple University Press, 1987; J. Haught, *The Cosmic Adventure: Science, Religion and the Quest for Purpose*, New York: Paulist Press, 1984; R.J. Russell, W.R. Stoeger, and G.Y. Coyne (eds.), *Physics, Philosophy and Theology: A Common Quest for Understanding*, Vatican City State, 1988.

18 S. Toulmin, *The Return to Cosmology: Post-Modern Science and the Theology of Nature*, Berkeley: University of California Press, 1982; D. Griffin (ed.), *The Re-enchantment of Science: Post-Modern Proposals*, New York: Suny Press, 1988; D. Griffin, *God and Religion in the Post-Modern World: Essays in Post-Modern Theology*, New York: Suny Press, 1989.

19 S. McDonagh, *To Care for the Earth*, London: Chapman, 1986; T. Berry, *The Dream of the Earth*, San Francisco: Sierra Book Club, 1988.

problem here is that cosmologies have come and gone at considerable speed in the last few centuries. However this must not become an excuse for refusing the dialogue, especially from a religion whose centre of gravity is the Word of God becoming flesh and entering into a new communion with human nature and with the world in which that human nature exists.

Initiating a Conversation between Cosmology and Christology

How then can we initiate this dialogue between cosmology and christology with a view to rediscovering the cosmic Christ? How can we move towards some appreciation of the cosmic significance of the Incarnation? What is the relationship of the Incarnation to creation?

The first point to note here is that such a dialogue is by no means something new to christianity, even though the dialogue may have broken down in a practical way over the last three centuries. A dialogue between christology and cosmology did in fact take place in the early centuries of christianity, especially through the Wisdom christology present in the Pauline corpus and the Synoptics, the Logos christology of St John, and the theology of the Greek Fathers. Indeed, it was partly the ability of christianity, especially in the first few centuries of its existence, to enter into a meaningful dialogue with the cosmology of the day, that enabled it to move from being a religion of particularity to being a religion of universal significance. The key to this growth, through the dialogue of early christianity with the surrounding culture, was the doctrine of the eternal Word/Logos of God incarnate in Jesus of Nazareth. The Word that was made flesh historically in Jesus was understood to be the definitive revelation of the same creative Word that made heaven and earth in the Book of Genesis and that was active in the history of Israel.

Among the Greek philosophers there was the recognition of a principle of reason/order/meaning/intelligibility which was understood to pervade the universe and this recognition existed since at least the fifth century BCE. In the second century AD, some would argue the first century AD, an important dialogue was initiated concerning the relationship of the incarnate Logos of John's Gospel and the logos of Greek philosophy. This dialogue, over a period of several centuries, gave rise to a clear recognition of Jesus as the personification of the Logos of Judaism and the logos of Greek cosmologies from Plato to middle Platonism and Stoicism. This recognition was registered formally at the Council of Nicea which defined Jesus 'of one being *(homoousios)* with God the Father' and which then went on to say that 'through the one Lord Jesus, the son of God, all things were made'. In effect, Jesus as the Word made flesh is the key to the meaning of history in Israel and the structured intelligibility of the universe in Greek philosophy.[20] Jaroslav Pelikan sums up this colourful period of dialogue between christianity and Greek philosophy in the following way:

> For by applying this title (Logos) to Jesus, the christian philosophers of the 4th and 5th centuries who were trying to give an account of who he was and what he had done were enabled to interpret him as the divine clue to the structure of reality (metaphysics) and, within metaphysics, to the riddle of being (ontology) – in a word, as the cosmic Christ.[21]

The foundation for this breakthrough was laid by the resurrection (Ac 1:10-11, Ac 2:32-36) and Wisdom (Ph 2:6-11; Rm 8:19-23; Ep 1:3-14; Col 1:15-20) christologies of the infant Church. This breakthrough that occurred in early christianity via dialogue with the different cosmologies is an important precedent and model for the conversation that should take place today between cosmology and christology.

Care must be taken not to set up false expectations or hopes concerning the outcome of the conversation between christology and cosmology. It would be theologically naive to expect contemporary cosmologies to be able to add new light to our understanding of christology just as it would be scientifically *simpliste* to think that christology could contribute new information

20 For some further details of this coming together of Greek philosophy and early christianity see D. Lane, *The Reality of Jesus: An Essay in Christology*, Dublin: Veritas Publications, 1975, ch. 7, esp. pp. 95-100.
21 *Jesus Through the Centuries*, op. cit.p. 58.

to the search of cosmology for a better understanding of the universe as a whole. Pushing the origins of the universe back some fifteen billion years does not alter substantially the questions about origins that theology has to face, though it must be admitted that the larger context does provoke a new kind of awe and wonder which are essential elements in any adequate theological response to these questions. The uneasy relationship between science and religion during the period of the enlightenment has at least taught important lessons in humility to both Jerusalem and Athens. At the same time it must be said that an open conversation between cosmology and christology could have a mutually enriching effect on their respective modes of understanding and praxis. It could also enable both disciplines to retrieve what may have been lost or forgotten within respective traditions. It could also help to moderate the claims of both areas by providing more inclusive points of reference.

Further, it must be noted that the proposed dialogue between christology and cosmology will not be achieved by making simple correlations between the past and the present. Recognition must be given to the cultural distance between early christianity and twentieth-century cosmologies. For example, the ancient cosmologies with which early christianity entered into dialogue are significantly different from the changing cosmologies of the twentieth century. The ancient cosmologies were by and large static, fixed and closed, whereas late twentieth-century cosmologies are dynamic, processive and open-ended.

Historians of cosmology now broadly distinguish three great eras in the history of cosmology: pre-modern, modern, and post-modern cosmologies. Pre-modern cosmologies, lasting up to the seventeenth century, were hierarchical, organic, patriarchal, static, fixed and respectful in their relationship towards nature. Modern cosmologies, from the seventeenth century to the middle of the twentieth century, have been mechanistic, materialistic, reductionist, atomistic and dominating in their relationship with nature. The third great era in cosmology, at present struggling to come to birth, is commonly called, for want of a better name, the post-modern era of cosmology.[22] The precise details of this post-modern cosmology have not yet been worked out in any coherent and consistent manner. If anything, post-modern cosmologies are more aware of what they stand for in terms of their reaction to, dissatisfaction with, and unease towards the modern cosmologies. As one post-modern cosmologist puts it:

> We no longer live in the modern world. The 'modern' world is now a thing of the past ... Natural science is no longer modern science. Instead it (natural science) is rapidly becoming a post-modern science ... The world has not yet discovered how it is to define itself in terms of what it is, but only in terms of what it has ceased to be.[23]

Yet, it is possible to say that the basic qualities of this emerging post-modern cosmology are organic, processive, inclusive, non-patriarchal, holistic and radically relational.

It is this newly emerging post-modern cosmology that we propose should become a conversation partner with christology in any attempt to rediscover the cosmic dimensions of the Incarnation. For that reason it is perhaps necessary to say something more about the shape, however tentative and provisional, of this post-modern cosmology.

A New Cosmic Story

One particular expression of the post-modern cosmology can be found in the writings of Tom Berry, who synthesises what is best in Teilhard de Chardin and the findings of contemporary science into what he calls a New Story.[24] According to Berry we need to remember that the vast universe as we know it through astronomy and astrophysics came into being some fifteen thousand million years ago. Some scientists talk about the origins of the universe in terms of 'the big bang theory' or 'the story of a cosmic explosion'. More significant is the suggestion that out of this extraordinary

22 Post-modern cosmologies are championed by such diverse authors as S. Toulmin, T. Berry, and D. Griffin whose works have already been mentioned in footnotes 18 and 19 above.
23 S. Toulmin, *The Recovery of Cosmology*, op. cit. p. 254.
24 See T. Berry, 'A New Story' in *The Dream of the Earth*, 1988. This New Story was originally published by T. Berry in *Teilhard Studies*, New York, winter 1978.

beginning, however this may be symbolised, there emerged over hundreds of millions of years the vast system of galaxies. These in turn gave rise to the earth, which in turn gave birth to the plants, animals and human life. Within this New Story a strong emphasis is placed on the fundamental unity that obtains between the galaxies, the earth, life forms and the emergence of human existence. Human existence is perceived as the earth in a particular mode of self-consciousness. The human person embodies the earth in a new condition of self-awareness and freedom. As Berry points out:

> We bear the universe in our beings as the universe bears us in its being.[25]

This arresting line of Berry's puts one in mind immediately of strikingly similar lines from Gerard Manley Hopkins:

> And what is earth's eye, tongue or heart else, where
> Else, but in dear and dogged man.[26]

What is significant about this New Story of the cosmos is the extraordinary unity that exists between the original 'fireball' and the evolutionary emergence of embodied self-consciousness via the galaxies, the solar system, the earth, and different life systems. According to the scientists we live in 'a finely tuned universe' which developed the particular way it did, in contrast to the many other possible outcomes, because it knew, as it were, that human beings were coming.[27]

A delicate balance of support and nurture exists between the universe, the earth and human existence, which at present is in danger of being seriously disrupted through ecological collapse. This balance is imaged in terms of 'a symphony of life' or 'a cosmic dance'. Within this New Story there is 'a growing awareness of the

---

25 T. Berry, op.cit, p. 132.
26 G. Manley Hopkins, 'Ribblesdale' *The Major Poems*, W. Davies (ed.), London: J.M. Dent, 1979, p. 88.
27 See D. Nicholl, 'At Home in the Universe', *The Tablet*, 23 April 1988, pp. 463-465. See also J. Barrow and F. Tipler, *The Anthropic Cosmological Principle*, Oxford: Oxford University Press, 1986.

physical/psychic dimension of reality'[28], of the 'withinness' and 'withoutness' of matter, the subjectivity and objectivity of the physical world which comes to full expression in the self-consciousness of the human person.

It is within the context of this New Story of cosmology that a new dialogue with christology might take place with a view to rediscovering the cosmic Christ. To be sure the New Story is quite incomplete and there are considerable differences when it comes to particular details. Yet there is sufficient agreement on the broad outlines of the new cosmic story to challenge and enrich christology. According to one physicist, Brian Swimme:

> For the first time in human existence, we have a cosmic story that is not tied to one cultural tradition, or to political ideology, but instead gathers every human group into its meaning ... Islamic people, Hopi people, Christian people, Marxist people and Hindu people can all agree in a basic sense on the birth of the sun, the development of the earth, the species of life, and human cultures.[29]

Dialogue from the Side of Christology

When we turn to the New Testament christology, we are struck immediately by the fact that one of the major points of reference, if not the major one, for understanding and interpreting Jesus is creation. The New Testament abounds with references to principalities and powers, heaven and earth, angels and spirits, stars and clouds, above and below – all of which are symbols of one kind or another referring to the cosmic context of the Christ-event. According to E. Schillebeeckx belief in creation is 'the all-supporting basis for the Jewish Christian Kerygma'.[30] One of the principal horizons of New Testament christology is creational and as such exists in stark contrast to the horizon of christological thinking from the seventeenth century to the twentieth century, during which it might be argued that our christology became too anthropocentric

---

28 T. Berry, *The Dream of the Earth*, op. cit. p. 133.
29 B. Swimme, 'The Cosmic Creation Story', *The Reenchantment of Science: Post Modern Proposals*, D. Griffin (ed.) New York: Suny Press, 1988, p. 52.
30 E. Schillebeeckx, *Christ*, London: SCM Press, 1980, p. 529.

and too ecclesiological. The missing link in modern christology has been the absence of a living cosmology. The emergence of a new cosmic story today is a challenge and an opportunity to redress this imbalance, not at the expense of a necessary anthropological and ecclesiological emphasis but to their mutual benefit.

A brief review of the titles of Jesus in New Testament christology reveals that many of them contain a direct connection with creation as their primary point of reference. We will confine ourselves here to three of these titles: Jesus as the Wisdom of God, Jesus as Lord, and Jesus as the eternal Logos.

Most commentators agree that one of the earliest christologies in the New Testament is that of Wisdom christology and that the identification of Jesus with Wisdom in the gospels and the Pauline corpus enabled christianity to assume cosmic significance early on.[31] The figure of Wisdom in the Hebrew and deuterocanonical scriptures is personal, female, and cosmic, having a functional equivalence with the activity of Yahweh in the self-understanding of Israel.[32] One clear reference to Jesus as the Wisdom of God is found in the First Letter of St Paul to the Corinthians:

> For the Jews demand signs and the Greeks seek wisdom, but we preach Christ crucified, a stumbling block to Jews and folly to the gentiles, but to those who are called, both Jew and gentile, Christ the power of God and the wisdom of God (1 Co 1:22-24).

For Paul, Jesus is the Wisdom of God and this identification of Jesus with the Wisdom of God links Jesus with the cosmic role of Wisdom in the Hebrew scriptures which is one of creating, caring and ordering the world and the affairs of history. Further on in the same Letter to the Corinthians Paul attributes explicitly some of the basic cosmic qualities of Wisdom from the Hebrew scriptures to Jesus:

---

31 See the helpful and important article by E.A. Johnson, 'Jesus, the Wisdom: A Biblical Basis for Non-anthrocentric Christology', in *Ephemerides Theologicae Lovanienses*, LXI (1985) 116-135; J. Dunne, *Christology in the Making: An Enquiry into the Origins of the Doctrine of the Incarnation*, London: SCM Press, 1980, ch. 6.
32   E.A. Johnson, op. cit., 263-276.

> For us there is one God, the Father, from whom are all things and for whom we exist, and one Lord Jesus Christ through whom we exist (1 Co 8:6).

The second half of this verse echoes many of the attributes of Wisdom contained in the Book of Proverbs and the Book of Wisdom.

An even greater concentration on the cosmic character of Jesus as the Wisdom of God can be found in Colossians 1:15-18:

> He is the image of the invisible God, the first born of all creation; for in him all things were created, in heaven and on earth, visible and invisible, whether thrones or dominions or principalities or authorities, all things were created through him and for him. He is before all things, and in him all things hold together.

Clearly the symbols in these verses are cosmic and much of the language parallels the language of the biblical Wisdom literature. What is instructive about this early Wisdom christology of the New Testament is the insistent reference to creation as the primary context for understanding the universal significance of the Christ-event.

Another equally important christology derives from the confession of Jesus as Lord (Rm 10:9, Ac 2:36). This title 'Lord' is both personal and cosmic in significance. Though it derives in origin from the social realm where someone who possesses authority and power over others is called 'Lord', it very quickly takes on cosmic significance in the light of the resurrection. Jesus is declared Lord in virtue of his exaltation which raises him up above the earth, sitting at the right hand of God the Father, giving him power over the whole of creation. Thus Jesus as Lord is divine ruler over the universe, taking on a kind of cosmic lordship. This is brought out in the christological hymn of Philippians which, significantly, is structured in the cosmology of the day that sees the world according to the threefold categories of heaven, earth and under the earth:

> And being found in human form he humbled himself ... Therefore God has highly exalted him and bestowed upon him the name which is above every name, that at the name of Jesus every knee shall bow, in heaven and on earth and under the earth, and every

tongue confess that Jesus Christ is Lord to the glory of God the Father (Ph 2:8-11).

The third example of a christology that takes creation as its primary point of reference is the Logos christology. The basic expression of a Logos christology is found in John's prologue, verses 1 to 16. In the Hebrew scriptures, 'the Word of God is God's utterance ... God's effective power ... God's rational energy reaching out into the world'.[33] The opening lines of John's prologue 'In the beginning was the Word ...' are intended to recall the opening words of the Book of Genesis: 'In the beginning God created the heavens and the earth'. The context, namely that of creation in the beginning, is the setting for the rest of John's prologue. The same creative Word of God that is active in the beginning is now the same creative Word that was made flesh in Jesus. The transition from creation to the historical event of Jesus is dramatic and the link between creation and Jesus is quickly established. The christology in the prologue of John's Gospel is creational and creation is itself christological. These New Testament christologies, situated in the context of creation, are a challenge to modern christology to rediscover its lost cosmic moorings.

A second aspect arising out of the conversation between cosmology and christology is the need to widen the terms of reference in the dialogue. Christological references to creation, in both the New Testament and subsequent theology, will have to begin to include not only the earth inhabited by human beings but also the whole of the universe. Given the indisputable linkage between human existence, the earth and the universe coming from the new cosmic story and the impossibility of understanding one without the other, it becomes necessary, for example, that discussions about the meaning of the Incarnation be seen to embrace not only the significance of the Incarnation for human existence but also for our understanding of the earth and the universe. Can we not say that the eternal Wisdom/Logos of God that became personally incarnate in Jesus, is the same divine Wisdom

33 J. Dunne, *Christology in the Making*, p. 248.

and Logos that is present nurturing and ordering life on the earth (see Gn 1, Pr 3:19; 8:22-31; Ws 7:22-8:1) and, equally, the same eternal Wisdom/Logos that nurtured, ordered and continues to hold together the cosmic process that began some fifteen billion years ago? Within this scheme of things we can begin to see a profound unity between the general involvement of God in the universe-earth-human process and the particular involvement of God in creation and Incarnation. The incarnation of Wisdom/Logos in Jesus is the coming into full glow of a cosmic process of divine self-communication set in motion millions upon millions of years ago. The Incarnation, therefore, is not some isolated divine intrusion that took place at one moment two thousand years ago but is rather the culmination and crystallisation of a divine cosmic process initiated at the dawn of time. The Incarnation was 'first' in God's intention – but not in time. Thus it becomes possible to say that from the beginning God was present in the universe-earth-human process and that the universe-earth-human process was present in God without however identifying God with the cosmos or the cosmos with God in a pantheistic way. Instead, we can adopt what some call a pan-en-theistic vision of God's presence in the organic reality of the universe, earth and human existence. This pan-en-theistic vision of God's presence in the world would seem to be implicit in a cosmic understanding of the Incarnation. A fundamental unity exists between the whole of creation and Incarnation; as we saw in chapter 2, the Mystery of Christ can be seen as a microcosm of what is taking place in the macrocosm of creation. A modern version of this can be found in Brian Swimme who suggests that:

> The human face is there in the structure of a fireball.[34]

The symbolic face present genetically as it were at the dawn of creation is the presence of divine Wisdom and the eternal Logos, that is the cosmic Christ, within the evolutionary process.

A third and final dimension emerging in the dialogue between

---

34 B. Swimme, 'Science: A Partner in Creating the Vision', *T. Berry and the New Cosmology*, A. Lonergan and C. Richards (eds.), Connecticut: Twenty-Third Publications, 1987, p. 88.

cosmology and christology concerns the presence of the cosmic Christ in the world today. So far we have been looking backwards from the Incarnation to creation. It is also possible, indeed necessary, to look forward from the Incarnation to the presence of Christ in the universe today. Taking the perception of the person coming from the New Story as the earth in a state of self-consciousness, could we not say that when the eternal Logos of God personally adopted human nature in Jesus, the Logos of God also adopted the earth and the universe in so far as these are actually embodied in the man Jesus. This would mean, in effect, that the Logos of God was and is personally present in the earth and in the universe. In the light of the Incarnation, therefore, the earth and the universe today assume special divine significance, analogous to the divine dignity of the person, deserving similar respect and reverence. There is something 'sacred', indeed sacramental, about the earth and the universe and their mutual processes in virtue of the Incarnation. Through the Incarnation God has taken 'matter' unto God's self. It is this awesome and sacramental quality of the earth and the universe at large that was lost since the time of the Enlightenment due to the absence of a living cosmology. The new dialogue between cosmology and christology should be able to restore a numinous, even a mystical quality to the whole of the living world as we know it today: human existence, the earth and the universe. David Tracy is surely pointing us in the right direction when he suggests that what is needed in theology today in the growing situation of a global pluralism is a rediscovery of the place of nature in history, a relocation of redemption in the context of creation and a recovery of the meaning of 'God' and 'self' in relation to the cosmos.[35]

A number of important theological consequences begin to flow from this initial conversation between cosmology and christology. These can only be mentioned in summary form here.

---

35 D. Tracy, 'Practical Theology in the Situation of Global Pluralism', *Formation and Reflection: The Promise of Practical Theology,* L.S. Mudge and J.N. Poling (eds.), Philadelphia: Fortress Press, 1987, pp. 146-152.

1. If we can begin to see the Wisdom and Logos of God that became incarnate in Jesus as something that was and is continually co-present in different degrees in the entire cosmic process, then the universe begins to appear a little more benign and friendly as a place to live in. In modern times, due to the demise of a living cosmology, the outer reaches of the universe appeared to many as cold, indifferent and even hostile. A dialogue between cosmology and christology which makes room for the involvement of the cosmic Christ from the beginning of time could reduce to some extent that sense of cosmic isolation and loneliness which arises from seeing the universe simply as a place without a purpose.

2. If, as a result of our conversation between cosmology and christology, we can begin to see the earth not as a machine but as a living organism which must be respected and revered, especially in virtue of the Incarnation, then there is some hope for the ecological movement. A rediscovery of the sacramental character of creation is a first step in the development of an appropriate theology of ecology. Humanity must not understand itself as existing objectively over and against the earth but rather as an integral part of the earth. This relocation of human identity within and not aloof from the living world of nature is an important step towards the preservation of the earth for the future. If a new alliance between humanity and the sacramentality of the earth can be established, then a new relationship between history and nature will begin to emerge. History and the so-called progress of history is not the right framework for cultivating the earth; instead the earth is an important part of a new framework for developing the history of humanity.[36]

3. If a cosmic christology helps us to rediscover the 'sacred' and therefore the sacramental character of the earth, then we have a richer context for a theology of the individual sacraments. Our disconnectedness from the earth, caused to a large degree by modern cosmologies, is partly responsible for the blunting of our

36 J. Moltmann, *God in Creation: A New Theology of Creation and the Spirit of God*, London: SCM Press, 1985, p. 56.

appreciation of the sacramental system. If, according to modern cosmologies, the world of matter is lifeless, then it becomes difficult to see how the matter of water and oil, bread and wine can become living symbols of God's saving and sacramental presence in Christ.

4. If our dialogue between cosmology and christology brings us back to cosmic origins, giving us a new sense of the unity of the universe, the earth and human existence, then it also propels us into the future towards conclusions. There is a growing awareness that origins and endings, though distinct, are nonetheless closely related. Equally there is an increasing awareness that the destiny of the individual is bound up with the destiny of the universe. More and more it is becoming clear that individual eschatology must be complemented by a cosmic eschatology. The conversation between cosmology and christology which points towards the cosmic Christ also points us in the direction of a cosmic eschatology.

To sum up, the Incarnation stands at the centre between creation and the consummation of creation in the eschaton. There is a fundamental unity between creation, Incarnation, and consummation. The ultimate 'centripetal force' of that unity is the crucified and risen Christ who is the Incarnation of the creative Wisdom/Logos of God holding all things together – past, present and to come. It is hardly surprising that it was a cosmologist, A.N. Whitehead, who with his keen sense of the presence of God pervading the cosmic processes, could write:

> The world lives by its incarnation of God in itself.[37]

Another way of capturing much of what we have been stammering to say concerning the human and cosmic dimensions of the Incarnation is given to us in the words of Elizabeth Barrett Browning:

---

37   A.N. Whitehead, *Religion in the Making*, New York, 1926, p. 151.

> Earth's crammed with heaven,
> And every common bush afire with God:
> But only he who sees
> Takes off his shoes.[38]

The final word, however, must be reserved for T.S. Eliot who captures and encapsulates the spirit of our reflections:

> These are only hints and guesses.
> Hints followed by guesses; and the rest
> Is prayer, observance, discipline, thought and action.
> The hint half guessed, the gift half understood, is Incarnation.[39]

---

38 'Auror Leigh', *Poetical Works of Elizabeth Barrett Browning*, New York: 1897, p. 466.
39 T.S. Eliot, 'The Dry Salvages', *Four Quartets.*

Select bibliography

Bredin, E., *Disturbing the Peace: The Way of Discipleship*, Dublin: Columba Press, 1985.

Brinkman, B., *To the Lengths of God: Truths and the Ecumenical Age*, London: SCM Press, 1988.

Carr, A., *Transforming Grace: Christian Tradition and Women's Experience*, San Francisco: Harper & Row, 1988.

Carroll, D., *A Pilgrim God for a Pilgrim People*, Dublin: Gill and Macmillan, 1988.

Chestnut, D.F., *Images of Christ: An Introduction to Christology*, New York: Seabury Press, 1984.

Daly, G., *Creation and Redemption*, Dublin: Gill and Macmillan, 1988.

Dunn, J., *Christology in the Making: A N.T. Enquiry into the Origins of the Doctrine of the Incarnation*, London: SCM Press, 1980.

Fiorenza, E.S., *In Memory of Her: A Feminist Theological Reconstruction of Christian Origins*, London: SCM Press, 1983.

Fitzmyer, *A Christological Catechism: New Testament Answers*, New York: Paulist Press, 1981.

Freyne, S., *Galilee, Jesus and the Gospels: Literary Approaches and Historical Investigations*. Dublin: Gill and Macmillan, 1988.

Kasper, W., *The God of Jesus Christ*, London: SCM Press, 1984.

Knitter, P., *No Other Name: A Critical Survey of Christian Attitudes towards World Religions*, London: SCM Press, 1985.

Krieg, R.A., *Story-Shaped Christology: The Role of Narrative in Identifying Jesus Christ*, New York: Paulist Press, 1988.

Mackey, J.P., *Modern Theology: A Sense of Direction*, Oxford: Oxford University Press, 1987.

Marthaler, B., *The Creed*, Connecticut: Twenty-Third Publications, 1987.

McDonagh, E., *The Gracing of Society*, Dublin: Gill and Macmillan, 1989.

McFague, S., *Models of God: Theology for an Ecological, Nuclear Age*, London: SCM Press, 1987.

Ogden, S., *The Point of Christology*, San Francisco: Harper & Row, 1982.

Pelikan, J., *Jesus Through the Centuries*, Newhaven and London: Yale University Press, 1985.

Ruether, R.R., *Sexism and God-talk: Towards a Feminist Theology*, London: SCM Press, 1983.

Schillebeeckx, E., *For the Sake of the Gospel*, London: SCM Press, 1989.

Shea, J., *The Spirit Master*, Chicago: Thomas More Press, 1987.

Sloyan, G.S., *Jesus in Focus: A Life in its Setting*, Connecticut: Twenty-Third Publications, 1983.

Sobrino, J., *Jesus in Latin America*, New York: Orbis Books, 1987.

Thompson, W.M., *The Jesus Debate: A Survey and Synthesis*, New York: Paulist Press, 1985.

Viviano, B., *The Kingdom of God in History*, Delaware: Michael Glazier Publications, 1988.

Willis, W. (ed.), *The Kingdom of God in 20th Century Interpretation*, Massachusetts: Hendrickson Publishers Inc., 1987.

Wilson-Kastner, P., *Faith, Feminism and the Christ*, Philadelphia: Fortress Press, 1983.

Index